Go Backend Engineering

Master Essential Techniques for Building Cloud-Native Applications with Golang

Corbin Husman

Table of Contents

Preface

Backend development is in constant flux, with new technologies and architectures emerging at a rapid pace. In this dynamic landscape, Go, or Golang, has emerged as a powerful and versatile language, perfectly suited for building modern, cloud-native applications. Its concurrency model, efficiency, and strong ecosystem have made it a favorite among developers seeking to create scalable and maintainable backend systems.

This book, "Go Backend Engineering: Master Essential Techniques for Building Cloud-Native Applications with Golang," is your comprehensive guide to mastering the art of backend development with Go. Whether you're a seasoned backend developer looking to expand your skillset or a newcomer eager to dive into the world of Go, this book will equip you with the knowledge and tools you need to succeed.

Within these pages, we embark on a journey that starts with the foundational elements of Go and progresses to advanced techniques for building robust, cloud-native applications. We'll explore core backend concepts, delve into Go's concurrency model, and master the art of building microservices. We'll navigate the complexities of cloud platforms, learn how to deploy and scale applications effectively, and discover best practices for security, testing, and performance optimization.

This book is not just about theory; it's about practical application. You'll find clear and concise code examples throughout, along with hands-on exercises and real-world case studies to reinforce your learning. We'll analyze production-ready codebases, dissect architectural patterns, and gain insights from experienced Go developers.

By the end of this book, you'll be able to:

- Confidently build RESTful APIs and microservices with Go.

- Harness the power of Go's concurrency model to create efficient and scalable applications.
- Deploy and manage Go applications on popular cloud platforms.
- Implement security best practices and protect against common vulnerabilities.
- Write clean, testable, and maintainable code.
- Optimize Go applications for performance in a cloud environment.

We believe that learning should be an engaging and enjoyable experience. Therefore, we've strived to present the material in a clear and accessible manner, with a focus on practical application and real-world relevance. We encourage you to experiment with the code, explore the concepts, and build your own Go backend applications.

As you embark on this journey of mastering Go backend engineering, we hope this book becomes your trusted companion, guiding you towards building exceptional cloud-native applications.

Chapter 1: Introduction to Backend Development

In this chapter, we'll lay the groundwork for your journey to becoming a proficient Go backend engineer. We'll explore why Go is an excellent choice for backend development, set up your development environment, and dive into the fundamentals of the Go language.

1.1 Why Go for Backend Development?

Go is becoming such a popular choice for building the engines that power our applications – the backend. You see, in the world of software, we often talk about the "frontend" (the part you see and interact with) and the "backend" (the behind-the-scenes logic and data management). And when it comes to building robust and efficient backends, Go has some compelling advantages.

Think of it this way: you're an architect designing a skyscraper. You wouldn't choose flimsy materials, would you? You need something strong, reliable, and able to handle immense weight and stress. Similarly, when choosing a programming language for your backend, you need something that can handle the demands of modern applications: processing massive amounts of data, responding to countless requests, and managing complex logic – all while remaining fast and stable.

This is where Go truly shines. Created by Google with these very needs in mind, Go, also known as Golang, offers a unique blend of features that make it a perfect fit for the challenges of backend development. Let's break down what makes Go so special:

1. Speed and Efficiency

Unlike interpreted languages that execute code line by line, Go is a *compiled* language. This means that before your Go program runs, a special tool called a compiler translates your code into machine instructions – the raw language that your computer's processor understands. This compilation process results in highly optimized executable files that run incredibly fast.

Why does this matter for backend development? Well, backend systems often handle a tremendous amount of work: processing user requests, fetching data from databases, performing calculations, and communicating with other services. The speed and efficiency of Go ensure that your backend can handle these tasks with lightning-fast response times, even under heavy load.

2. Concurrency: Handling Multiple Tasks with Grace

Modern applications are like bustling cities, with countless activities happening simultaneously. Users are logging in, submitting forms, making purchases, and interacting with various features all at the same time. To handle this constant flurry of activity, your backend needs to be able to multitask effectively.

Go excels at this thanks to its built-in support for *concurrency*. It provides lightweight, independent execution units called "goroutines" that allow your program to perform multiple tasks concurrently. Think of goroutines as highly efficient workers who can handle different parts of a job simultaneously, without getting in each other's way.

Go also provides "channels," which are like communication pipelines between goroutines. Channels enable safe and efficient data exchange between these concurrent workers, ensuring that your application remains organized and synchronized even when handling a multitude of tasks.

This inherent concurrency support makes Go ideal for building applications that need to handle many simultaneous requests, process large datasets, or interact with multiple services concurrently.

3. Simplicity and Readability: Code that's Easy to Understand

Go was designed with a clear philosophy: simplicity and readability. Its syntax is clean, straightforward, and easy to grasp, even for developers coming from other languages. This means you can spend less time deciphering complex code and more time building and innovating.

Moreover, Go's focus on readability promotes better collaboration among developers. When code is easy to understand, it's easier to review, maintain, and debug, leading to more robust and reliable applications.

4. Strong Ecosystem

Imagine you're a chef preparing a grand feast. You wouldn't want to start from scratch with every ingredient, would you? You'd rely on pre-made sauces, spices, and tools to speed up your work and enhance your creations. Similarly, in the world of programming, a strong ecosystem of libraries and tools can significantly boost your productivity and efficiency.

Go boasts a vibrant and growing ecosystem, with a wide range of libraries and frameworks readily available for common backend tasks. Need to connect to a database? There's a library for that. Want to build a web server? There's a package for that too. From handling JSON data to implementing authentication, Go's ecosystem provides the building blocks you need to construct powerful and feature-rich backend systems.

5. Cloud-Native Fit: Built for Modern Infrastructure

Today's applications often live in the cloud, running on platforms like Amazon Web Services (AWS), Google Cloud Platform (GCP), or Microsoft Azure. These cloud environments demand applications that are lightweight, efficient, and easily scalable.

Go is a perfect fit for this cloud-native world. Its small memory footprint and fast execution speed make it ideal for containerization technologies like Docker, which package applications into portable units for easy deployment. Go also plays well with orchestration systems like Kubernetes, which automate the deployment, scaling, and management of containerized applications.

Real-World Examples:

To illustrate Go's prowess in backend development, let's look at some real-world examples:

- Docker: The core of Docker, the popular containerization platform, is written in Go. Go's efficiency and concurrency features make it ideal for managing containers and orchestrating their interactions.
- Kubernetes: Kubernetes, the leading container orchestration system, is also built with Go. Go's ability to handle complex logic and network communication makes it a perfect choice for managing large-scale deployments.
- Dropbox: Dropbox, the popular file-sharing service, migrated some of its performance-critical backend components from Python to Go, resulting in significant improvements in speed and efficiency.
- Netflix: Netflix utilizes Go in its server architecture to handle massive amounts of streaming data and ensure a smooth viewing experience for millions of users.

These examples demonstrate how Go is being used to power some of the most demanding and high-traffic applications in the world.

A Simple Code Example:

Let's see a simple Go program that demonstrates its basic syntax and how to use the fmt package for printing output:

Go

```
package main

import "fmt"

func main() {

    name := "Alice"

    age := 30

    fmt.Println("Hello,", name)

    fmt.Println("You are", age, "years old.")

}
```

In this code:

- package main indicates that this is the main program file.
- import "fmt" imports the fmt package, which provides functions for formatted input and output.
- func main() is the main function where the program execution begins.
- name := "Alice" declares a variable named name and assigns it the string value "Alice."
- age := 30 declares a variable named age and assigns it the integer value 30.
- fmt.Println(...) prints the given values to the console.

When you run this program, it will print:

Hello, Alice

You are 30 years old.

This simple example gives you a glimpse of Go's clean syntax and how easy it is to work with basic data types and output.

Go offers a powerful combination of speed, concurrency, simplicity, and a thriving ecosystem, making it a compelling choice for building modern, cloud-native backend systems. As you progress through this book, you'll gain a deeper understanding of these features and learn how to leverage them to build your own high-performance backend applications.

1.2 Setting Up Your Go Environment

Let's set up your Go development environment. Think of this as preparing your workspace with all the necessary tools and equipment before starting a new project. Fortunately, setting up Go is a straightforward process, and I'll guide you through it step-by-step.

1. Download and Install Go

First things first, we need to get Go installed on your system. Head over to the official Go website (https://golang.org) and download the appropriate installer for your operating system (Windows, macOS, or Linux). The website will automatically detect your OS and recommend the correct download.

Once the download is complete, run the installer and follow the on-screen instructions. The installer will guide you through the installation process,[1] which typically involves accepting the license agreement and choosing the installation directory. In most cases, the default settings will work just fine.

2. Verify the Installation

After the installation is finished, it's always a good idea to verify that everything is set up correctly. Open your terminal or command prompt (depending on your operating system) and type the following command:

Bash

```
go version
```

If Go is installed correctly, you should see the installed version printed on the console, like this:

```
go version go1.20.4 linux/amd64
```

This confirms that Go is ready to use on your system.

3. Set Your GOPATH

Now, let's talk about the GOPATH. This is an environment variable that tells Go where to find your workspaces – the directories where you'll store your Go projects and downloaded packages.

You have the freedom to set your GOPATH to any directory you prefer. A common practice is to create a dedicated directory called go within your home directory. For example, on Linux or macOS, you might use the following path:

```
$HOME/go
```

To set the GOPATH environment variable, you'll need to add a line to your shell's configuration file. This file is typically named .bashrc or .zshrc on Linux/macOS and is located in your home directory. Open this file in a text editor and add the following line, replacing $HOME/go with your chosen GOPATH directory:

Bash

```
export GOPATH=$HOME/go
```

After saving the file, you need to either close and reopen your terminal or run the following command to apply the changes:

Bash

```
source ~/.bashrc   # or source ~/.zshrc
```

Now, when you run go commands, Go will know where to find your workspaces and packages.

4. Choose a Code Editor or IDE

While you can technically write Go code in any plain text editor, using a code editor or an Integrated Development Environment (IDE) with Go support can significantly enhance your productivity. These tools provide features like syntax highlighting, code completion, debugging, and code formatting, which make writing and debugging Go code much easier.

Here are some popular choices for Go development:

- Visual Studio Code (VS Code): This is a free, lightweight, and highly extensible code editor that has excellent Go support through the official Go extension. It's a popular choice among Go developers due to its versatility and customization options.
- GoLand: This is a full-featured, commercial IDE specifically designed for Go development by JetBrains. It offers advanced features like intelligent code completion, refactoring tools, and integrated debugging, making it a powerful choice for professional Go development.
- Sublime Text: This is another popular code editor known for its speed and customization options. It has good Go support through community-maintained packages.

The choice of editor or IDE ultimately comes down to personal preference. I recommend trying out a few options to see which one best fits your workflow and preferences.

5. Install Necessary Extensions

If you choose to use an editor like VS Code, you'll need to install the official Go extension to get the best Go development experience. This extension provides a wealth of features, including:

- Code Completion: As you type, the extension suggests possible completions for variables, functions, and keywords, helping you write code faster and with fewer errors.
- Code Navigation: Easily jump to definitions of functions and variables, navigate between files, and explore your codebase.
- Debugging: Set breakpoints, step through your code, and inspect variables to identify and fix bugs effectively.
- Code Formatting: Automatically format your code to adhere to Go's style guidelines, ensuring consistency and readability.

To install the Go extension in VS Code, open the Extensions view (Ctrl+Shift+X), search for "Go", and click the "Install" button.

A Quick Test Drive

Now that you have your Go environment set up, let's take it for a quick test drive. Create a new directory for your Go projects within your GOPATH. For example:

```
mkdir $GOPATH/src/my-go-project
```

Inside this directory, create a file named main.go and paste the following code:

```Go
package main

import "fmt"

func main() {

  fmt.Println("Hello, Go!")

}
```

Open your terminal, navigate to the my-go-project directory, and run the following command:

```Bash

go run main.go
```

You should see "Hello, Go!" printed on your console. Congratulations! You've just run your first Go program.

With your Go environment set up and a successful test run under your belt, you're ready to embark on your Go backend development journey. In the next section, we'll start exploring the fundamentals of the Go language, laying the foundation for building powerful and efficient backend applications.

1.3 Understanding Go Basics

Now that your Go workspace is set up, let's discuss the foundational elements of the Go language itself. Think of this as learning the grammar and vocabulary of Go, the building blocks you'll use to construct your backend applications. We'll cover the essential aspects of Go syntax, data types, and control flow, providing you with a solid understanding of how Go programs are structured and executed.

Syntax

Just like any language, Go has its own set of rules and conventions – its syntax. These rules dictate how you write code that the Go compiler can understand and translate into executable instructions. Let's look at some key aspects of Go syntax:

- Case-Sensitivity: Go is a case-sensitive language. This means that uppercase and lowercase letters are treated as distinct. So, a variable named userName is different from a variable named username. This distinction might seem minor, but it's crucial for writing correct Go code.

- Semicolons: In many programming languages, you need to end each statement with a semicolon (;). However, Go is more forgiving in this regard. You typically don't need semicolons at the end of statements. The Go compiler is smart enough to infer the end of a statement in most cases. However, semicolons are still allowed, and you might encounter them in some codebases.
- Curly Braces: Curly braces {} play a crucial role in Go. They are used to define code blocks, which are groups of statements that are executed together. In Go, curly braces are mandatory even if the code block contains only a single statement. This enforces consistency and readability in your code.

Data Types

In the world of programming, data types are like containers that hold different kinds of information. Go provides a variety of built-in data types to represent various forms of data:

- Basic Types: These are the fundamental data types in Go:
  - int: Represents integer values (whole numbers), such as 10, -5, or 1000.
  - float64: Represents floating-point numbers (numbers with decimal points), such as 3.14, -2.5, or 0.001.
  - string: Represents textual data, such as "Hello, Go!" or "This is a string."
  - bool: Represents boolean values, which can be either true or false. These are often used for making decisions in your code.
- Composite Types: These data types allow you to group and organize data in various ways:

- array: Represents a fixed-size collection of elements of the same data type. For example, an array of integers could store the ages of students in a class.
- slice: Provides a more flexible way to work with collections of elements. Slices can grow or shrink in size as needed.
- map: Stores key-value pairs, allowing you to associate a value with a specific key. Think of a dictionary where you look up a word (key) to find its definition (value).
- struct: Allows you to create custom data structures by combining different data types. For example, you could define a struct to represent a customer with fields like name, address, and phone number.

Control Flow

Control flow statements determine the order in which your code is executed. They allow you to make decisions, repeat actions, and control the overall flow of your program.

- Conditional Statements: These statements allow your program to execute different blocks of code based on certain conditions.
  - if: Executes a block of code if a condition is true.
  - else if:[1] Provides an alternative condition to check if the previous if condition is false.
  - else: Executes a block of code if none of the preceding if or else if conditions are true.
- Loops: Loops allow you to repeat a block of code multiple times.
  - for: The most common loop in Go. It allows you to specify a condition and a block of code to execute repeatedly as long as the condition remains true.

- Switch Statement: The switch statement provides a concise way to select one of many code blocks to execute based on the value of an expression.

Code Example: Calculating a Discount

Let's see a practical example of how to use data types and control flow in Go. Consider a scenario where you need to calculate a discount based on the purchase amount:

```Go
package main

import "fmt"

func main() {

    purchaseAmount := 150.00

    discount := 0.0

    if purchaseAmount >= 100 {

        discount = 0.10 // 10% discount

    } else if purchaseAmount >= 50 {

        discount = 0.05 // 5% discount

    }

    finalAmount := purchaseAmount - (purchaseAmount * discount)

    fmt.Println("Final amount after discount:", finalAmount)

}
```

In this code:

- We declare a variable purchaseAmount of type float64 to store the purchase amount.
- We use an if-else if statement to determine the discount based on the purchaseAmount.
- We calculate the finalAmount after applying the discount.
- We use fmt.Println to print the final amount to the console.

This example demonstrates how you can use data types to represent numerical values and control flow statements to make decisions in your Go code.

Exercise: Checking for Even or Odd

Now, try this exercise to test your understanding of control flow:

Write a Go program that takes an integer as input and prints whether it's even or odd.

Real-World Example: User Authentication

In a real-world backend application, you might use control flow to implement user authentication. For example, you could use an if statement to check if the user has entered the correct password before granting them access to a protected resource.

As you can see, understanding Go's syntax, data types, and control flow is fundamental to writing effective Go programs. These concepts form the bedrock upon which you'll build more complex and sophisticated backend applications. In the next section, we'll explore how Go code is organized into packages and modules, allowing you to structure your projects effectively and reuse code efficiently.

1.4 Working with Packages and Modules

As you start building larger and more complex Go applications, you'll quickly realize the importance of organizing your code effectively. This is where packages and modules come into play. They provide a structured way to manage your codebase, promote reusability, and make collaboration with other developers smoother. Let's discuss how packages and modules work in Go.

Packages

Think of packages as containers for related code. They help you group functions, variables, and other code elements into logical units, making your codebase more organized and easier to navigate. In essence, packages provide a way to create modular and reusable components within your Go projects.

Every Go program starts with a package main. This special package indicates that the code in this file is the entry point for your application – the place where execution begins. Within the main package, you'll typically have a main() function, which serves as the starting point for your program's logic.

Beyond the main package, you can create your own custom packages to organize different parts of your application. For example, you might have a package called users to handle user-related functionality (like user registration, login, and profile management), a package called products to manage product data, and a package called orders to handle order processing.

Importing Packages

To use code from other packages, you need to import them into your Go file. This is done using the import keyword followed by the package path enclosed in double quotes. For example, to use the fmt package (which provides functions for formatted input and output), you would import it like this:

Go

```go
import "fmt"
```

Once a package is imported, you can access its exported functions and variables using the package name followed by a dot (.). For instance, to use the Println function from the fmt package, you would write:

Go

```go
fmt.Println("Hello, Go!")
```

Modules:

In modern software development, it's common to rely on external libraries and frameworks to avoid reinventing the wheel. These external codebases are often referred to as dependencies. In Go, modules provide a way to manage these dependencies effectively.

A module is a collection of packages that are versioned and released together. Think of it as a bundle of related code that you can include in your project. Modules help you:

- Manage Dependencies: Modules clearly define the external packages your project relies on, making it easier to track and update them.
- Versioning: Modules allow you to specify the exact version of a dependency you want to use, ensuring consistency and avoiding conflicts.
- Code Reusability: Modules promote code reusability by allowing you to easily share and reuse packages across different projects.

Creating a Module

To create a new module for your Go project, you use the go mod init command followed by the module path. The module path is a unique identifier for your module, typically in the form of a domain name or a repository URL. For example:

```bash
Bash

go mod init
github.com/your-username/my-go-project
```

This command creates a go.mod file in your project directory. The go.mod file serves as the module definition, listing the module path, the Go version used, and the project's dependencies.

Adding Dependencies

When you use an external package in your Go code, Go automatically adds it as a dependency to your go.mod file. You can also manually add dependencies using the go get command followed by the package path. For example, to add the gorilla/mux package (a popular routing library), you would run:

```bash
Bash

go get github.com/gorilla/mux
```

This command downloads the gorilla/mux package and adds it to your go.mod file.

Code Example: Using a Third-Party Package

Let's see an example of how to use a third-party package in your Go code. We'll use the gorilla/mux package to create a simple web server with routing:

```go
Go

package main

import (
```

```go
    "fmt"

    "net/http"

    "github.com/gorilla/mux"
)

func homeHandler(w http.ResponseWriter, r *http.Request) {

    fmt.Fprintln(w, "Welcome to the homepage!")

}

func aboutHandler(w http.ResponseWriter, r *http.Request) {

    fmt.Fprintln(w, "This is the about page.")

}

func main() {

    router := mux.NewRouter()

    router.HandleFunc("/", homeHandler)

    router.HandleFunc("/about", aboutHandler)

    fmt.Println("Server listening on port 8080")

    http.ListenAndServe(":8080", router)

}
```

In this code:

- We import the net/http package for web server functionality and the github.com/gorilla/mux package for routing.

- We define two handler functions, homeHandler and aboutHandler, to handle requests to different routes.
- We create a new router using mux.NewRouter().
- We use router.HandleFunc to map routes to their respective handlers.
- We start the web server using http.ListenAndServe.

This example demonstrates how you can leverage external packages to add functionality to your Go applications.

Real-World Example: Building a REST API

In a real-world scenario, you might use packages and modules to build a REST API for an e-commerce application. You could have separate packages for handling user authentication, product management, order processing, and payment integration. Each of these packages could be organized as a module, allowing you to reuse them across different projects or even share them with the wider Go community.

1.5 Essential Standard Library Packages

One of Go's greatest strengths is its robust standard library – a collection of pre-built packages that provide a wide range of functionalities. Think of it as a toolbox filled with ready-to-use tools for various tasks. For backend development, several standard library packages are particularly essential. Let's explore these packages and see how they can help you build powerful and efficient backend systems.

1. fmt : Formatting Input and Output

The fmt package is your gateway to interacting with the outside world – displaying information on the console, formatting strings, and reading user input. It's like the communication hub of your Go programs.

Here are some of the key functions provided by the fmt package:

- **Println(...):** This function prints a line of text to the console. You can pass it any number of values of different types, and it will automatically format them and print them on a new line.
- **Printf(...):** This function allows you to print formatted output. You can use format specifiers (like %d for integers, %f for floating-point numbers, and %s for strings) to control how the output is displayed.
- **Sprintf(...):** This function is similar to Printf, but instead of printing the output to the console, it returns the formatted string. This is useful when you need to construct strings dynamically.
- **Scanln(...):** This function reads user input from the console. You provide variables to store the input values, and Scanln will read the input and assign it to those variables.

Code Example: Formatting Output

```Go
package main

import "fmt"

func main() {

  name := "Alice"

  age := 30

  fmt.Println("Hello,", name)

  fmt.Printf("You are %d years old.\n", age)

  message := fmt.Sprintf("Welcome, %s!", name)
```

```
fmt.Println(message)
```

```
}
```

This code demonstrates how to use Println, Printf, and Sprintf to print formatted output to the console.

2. net/http: Building Web Servers and Handling Requests

The net/http package is the cornerstone of web development in Go. It provides the tools you need to build web servers, handle HTTP requests, and create APIs that communicate with other systems.

Here are some of the key components of the net/http package:

- http.HandleFunc(...): This function allows you to register handler functions for specific URL paths. When a request arrives for a particular path, the associated handler function is executed.
- http.ListenAndServe(...): This function starts a web server that listens on a specified port (e.g., :8080) and handles incoming requests.
- http.Request: This struct represents an incoming HTTP request. It contains information about the request method (GET, POST, etc.), headers, URL, and request body.
- http.ResponseWriter: This interface allows you to send HTTP responses back to the client. You can use it to set headers, write the response body, and set the status code.

Code Example: A Simple Web Server

```Go
package main

import (
```

```go
    "fmt"

    "net/http"

)

func handler(w http.ResponseWriter, r
*http.Request) {

    fmt.Fprintln(w, "Hello from the web server!")

}

func main() {

    http.HandleFunc("/", handler)

    fmt.Println("Server listening on port 8080")

    http.ListenAndServe(":8080", nil)

}
```

This code creates a simple web server that listens on port 8080 and responds with "Hello from the web server!" to any request.

3. encoding/json: **Working with JSON Data**

JSON (JavaScript Object Notation) is a widely used data format for exchanging information between web servers and clients. The encoding/json package provides functions for encoding Go data structures into JSON format and decoding JSON data into Go data structures.

Here are some of the important functions in the encoding/json package:

- json.Marshal(...): This function takes a Go data structure (like a struct or a map) and converts it into a JSON-formatted byte slice.
- json.Unmarshal(...): This function takes a JSON-formatted byte slice and converts it into a Go data structure.

Code Example: Encoding and Decoding JSON

```go
Go

package main

import (

  "encoding/json"

  "fmt"

)

type User struct {

  Name   string `json:"name"`

  Age    int    `json:"age"`

  Email string `json:"email"`

}

func main() {

  user := User{Name: "Alice", Age: 30, Email:
"alice@example.com"}

  jsonData, _ := json.Marshal(user)
```

```go
    fmt.Println(string(jsonData)) // Output:
{"name":"Alice","age":30,"email":"alice@example.c
om"}

    var decodedUser User

    json.Unmarshal(jsonData, &decodedUser)

    fmt.Println(decodedUser) // Output: {Alice 30
alice@example.com}

}
```

This code demonstrates how to encode a Go struct into JSON format and decode JSON data back into a Go struct.

4. database/sql: Interacting with SQL Databases

Most backend applications rely on databases to store and retrieve data. The database/sql package provides a generic interface for interacting with SQL databases (like PostgreSQL, MySQL, and SQLite).

This package allows you to:

- Connect to a database.
- Execute SQL queries.
- Retrieve query results.
- Manage database transactions.

5. os: Interacting with the Operating System

The os package provides functions for interacting with the underlying operating system. This includes:

- File system operations (creating, reading, writing, and deleting files).
- Environment variables.
- Process management.

6. sync: **Synchronizing Concurrent Operations**

When working with concurrency in Go (using goroutines), you often need to synchronize access to shared resources to prevent race conditions. The sync package provides tools like mutexes and wait groups to help you manage concurrency safely.

7. io: **Input and Output Operations**

The io package provides a set of interfaces for performing input and output operations, such as reading from and writing to files, network connections, and other data streams.

Real-World Example: Building an E-commerce Backend

In a real-world e-commerce application, you might use:

- net/http to create a REST API for handling product listings, orders, and payments.
- encoding/json to encode and decode JSON data exchanged with the frontend.
- database/sql to interact with a database to store product information, user data, and order details.
- os to access configuration files or log errors to files.
- sync to synchronize access to shared resources like shopping carts.

These standard library packages provide the foundational tools for building a wide range of backend applications. As you become more familiar with Go, you'll discover even more packages in the standard library that can help you solve specific problems and build robust and efficient backend systems.

Chapter 2: Core Backend Concepts

In this chapter, we'll explore the core concepts that underpin how backend systems work. We'll uncover the magic behind web servers, APIs, and how your Go applications can communicate with the rest of the digital world.

2.1 Client-Server Model and HTTP

Let's talk about how the internet works, specifically the communication that happens behind the scenes whenever you use a web application. At the heart of this communication lies a fundamental concept called the **client-server model**.

Think of it like this: you're at a restaurant, and you're hungry. You (the **client**) have a menu (the user interface), and you decide what you want to eat. You then place your order with the waiter (the **server**). The waiter takes your order to the kitchen, where the chefs prepare your food (process your request).[1] Once the food is ready, the waiter brings it back to you (delivers the response).[2]

In the digital world, the client-server model works similarly.[3] You, with your web browser or mobile app, are the client.[4] You make requests for information or actions, such as viewing a webpage, submitting a form, or making a purchase.[5] The server, a powerful computer located somewhere else, receives your requests, processes them, and sends back the appropriate response.[6]

This communication between clients and servers happens through a protocol called **HTTP (Hypertext Transfer Protocol)**.[7] It's like a standardized language that both clients and servers understand, allowing them to exchange information in a structured and reliable way.

How HTTP Works

HTTP relies on a request-response cycle.[8] Here's a breakdown of how it works:

1. Request: You type a URL into your web browser (e.g., www.example.com/products). Your browser sends an HTTP request to the server hosting that website, asking for the web page located at that URL.[9] This request includes information like:
   o Method: The type of request (e.g., GET to retrieve data, POST to submit data).
   o Headers: Metadata about the request, such as the browser you're using, the types of content you can accept, and any cookies associated with the website.[10]
   o Body: Optional data sent with the request, such as form data or JSON payload.[11]
2. Processing: The server receives your request and examines it.[12] It uses the information in the request to determine what action to take.[13] For example, if the request is for /products, the server might query a database to retrieve a list of products.
3. Response: Once the server has processed the request, it sends back an HTTP response.[14] This response includes:
   o Status Code: A numerical code indicating the outcome of the request (e.g., 200 OK for success, 404 Not Found if the resource wasn't found).
   o Headers: Metadata about the response, such as the content type (e.g., text/html for a webpage, application/json for JSON data).
   o Body: The actual data being sent back, such as the HTML content of a webpage or a JSON representation of a list of products.
4. Rendering: Your browser receives the response and interprets it.[15] If the response is a web page, the browser renders the HTML content, displaying the page on your screen.[16] If the response is JSON data, your browser might

use it to update parts of the page or pass it to a JavaScript application for further processing.

HTTP Methods

HTTP defines several methods for different types of requests:[17]

- GET: Used to retrieve data from the server.[18] For example, fetching a web page, getting a list of products, or retrieving a user's profile.
- POST: Used to submit data to the server to create a new resource.[19] For example, submitting a form to create a new user account, adding a product to a shopping cart, or posting a comment.[20]
- PUT: Used to update an existing resource on the server.[21] For example, updating a user's profile information or modifying the details of a product.
- DELETE: Used to delete a resource from the server.[22] For example, deleting a user account or removing a product from a catalog.

These methods, along with URLs and headers, provide a standardized way for clients and servers to communicate and exchange information over the internet.

Real-World Examples

The client-server model and HTTP are the foundation of countless web applications you use every day:

- Online Shopping: When you browse an online store, add items to your cart, and make a purchase, you're interacting with a web server that manages product information, inventory, and your shopping session.[23]
- Social Media: Social media platforms rely on the client-server model to handle user interactions, posts, likes,

and comments.[24] Your phone or computer acts as the client, communicating with the social media company's servers to display content and update your feed.[25]

- Banking: Online banking systems use the client-server model to provide secure access to your account information, allow you to make transactions, and view your statements.
- Streaming Services: When you watch a movie on Netflix or listen to music on Spotify, your device acts as the client, requesting video or audio streams from the streaming service's servers.[26]

Code Example: A Basic HTTP Server in Go

Go's standard library provides the net/http package, which makes it easy to build web servers and handle HTTP requests. Here's a simple example of a Go program that creates a basic HTTP server:

```Go
package main

import (

  "fmt"

  "net/http"

)

func handler(w http.ResponseWriter, r *http.Request) {

  fmt.Fprintln(w, "Hello from the Go web server!")

}

func main() {
```

```
    http.HandleFunc("/", handler) // Register the
handler function for the root path ("/")

    fmt.Println("Server listening on port 8080")

    http.ListenAndServe(":8080", nil) // Start the
server on port 8080

}
```

In this code:

- We import the net/http package.
- We define a handler function that takes two arguments: http.ResponseWriter (for sending responses) and http.Request (for accessing request information).
- We use http.HandleFunc("/", handler) to register the handler function for the root path ("/"). This means that when a client makes a request to localhost:8080/, this handler will be executed.
- We use http.ListenAndServe(":8080", nil) to start the web server on port 8080.

If you run this code and visit localhost:8080 in your web browser, you'll see the message "Hello from the Go web server!" displayed on the page.

This example demonstrates the basic structure of a Go web server and how to handle HTTP requests. As you progress through this book, you'll learn how to build more complex and feature-rich web applications using Go.

2.2 Building RESTful APIs with Go

Let's talk about how you can use Go to build powerful and efficient APIs that allow different applications to communicate and exchange data. We'll focus on a popular architectural style called REST, which stands for Representational State Transfer. REST provides a set of guidelines and conventions for designing APIs that are scalable, flexible, and easy to use.

What is a RESTful API?

Think of a RESTful API as a waiter in a restaurant. You (the client) give your order (a request) to the waiter (the API), who then takes it to the kitchen (the server), gets your food (data), and brings it back to you (the response).

In a RESTful API, you use standard HTTP methods (like GET, POST, PUT, and DELETE) to interact with resources. A resource can be anything – a user, a product, an article, or any other piece of data that your application manages. Each resource is identified by a unique URL (Uniform Resource Locator), which is like its address on the web.

For example, if you're building an API for an online store, you might have resources like:

- /products: Represents the collection of all products.
- /products/123: Represents the product with ID 123.
- /users: Represents the collection of all users.
- /users/456: Represents the user with ID 456.

Key Principles of REST

RESTful APIs adhere to a set of key principles:

- Client-Server Architecture: REST APIs follow the client-server model, where clients make requests and servers provide responses. This separation of concerns allows for independent evolution of the client and server components.
- Statelessness: Each request from the client to the server must contain all the information necessary to understand and process the request. The server does not store any client[1] context between requests. This makes RESTful APIs

scalable and reliable, as servers can handle requests independently without relying on previous interactions.

- Cacheability: Responses from the server should explicitly state whether they can be cached or not. This allows clients (or intermediary servers) to cache responses, reducing the number of requests to the server and improving performance.
- Uniform Interface: RESTful APIs use a uniform interface for interacting with resources. This interface relies on standard HTTP methods (GET, POST, PUT, DELETE), URLs for identifying resources, and standard data formats (like JSON) for representation.
- Layered System: Clients should not be able to tell whether they are connected directly to the end server or an intermediary server (like a load balancer). This allows for flexibility in the architecture and deployment of RESTful APIs.

Building RESTful APIs with Go

Go's net/http package provides the foundation for building RESTful APIs. You can define handler functions for different HTTP methods and URL paths, and the net/http package takes care of routing the requests to the appropriate handlers.

Here's a simple example of a Go program that creates a RESTful API for managing users:

```Go
package main

import (

  "encoding/json"

  "fmt"
```

```go
    "net/http"
)

type User struct {
    ID    int    `json:"id"`
    Name string `json:"name"`
    Email string `json:"email"`
}

func getUsersHandler(w http.ResponseWriter, r
*http.Request) {
    // ... (code to fetch all users from a
database) ...
    users := []User{
        {ID: 1, Name: "Alice", Email:
"alice@example.com"},
        {ID: 2, Name: "Bob", Email:
"bob@example.com"},
    } // Replace with actual user data
    w.Header().Set("Content-Type",
"application/json")
    json.NewEncoder(w).Encode(users)
}

func createUserHandler(w http.ResponseWriter, r
*http.Request) {
```

```go
    // ... (code to decode JSON request body and
create a new user in the database) ...

    w.WriteHeader(http.StatusCreated) // Send a 201
Created status code

}

func main() {

    http.HandleFunc("/users", getUsersHandler)

    http.HandleFunc("/users",
createUserHandler).Methods("POST") // Handle POST
requests to /users

    fmt.Println("Server listening on port 8080")

    http.ListenAndServe(":8080", nil)

}
```

In this code:

- We define a User struct to represent a user.
- We define a getUsersHandler function to handle GET requests to /users. This function fetches all users from the database (represented here by a placeholder user's slice) and sends them back as a JSON response.
- We define a createUserHandler function to handle POST requests to /users. This function would decode the JSON request body, create a new user in the database, and send a success response.
- We use http.HandleFunc("/users", getUsersHandler) to register the getUsersHandler for GET requests to /users.
- We use http.HandleFunc("/users", createUserHandler).Methods("POST") to register the createUserHandler specifically for POST requests to /users.

This example demonstrates the basic structure of a RESTful API in Go. You can expand this API to include more endpoints for retrieving individual users, updating users, deleting users, and performing other actions.

Real-World Examples

RESTful APIs are used extensively in modern web applications:

- E-commerce Platforms: Online stores use REST APIs to manage product catalogs, handle orders, process payments, and provide user accounts.
- Social Media Networks: Social media platforms use REST APIs to allow users to post updates, like content, and connect with friends.
- Cloud Services: Cloud providers like AWS, GCP, and Azure offer REST APIs for managing cloud resources, such as virtual machines, databases, and storage.
- Mobile Apps: Mobile apps often communicate with backend servers through REST APIs to fetch data, synchronize information, and perform actions.

2.3 Handling HTTP Requests and Responses

In Go, the net/http package provides the tools you need to work with HTTP requests and responses. When a client (like a web browser or a mobile app) sends an HTTP request to your Go server, the net/http package gives you two essential objects to work with:

1. http.Request

The http.Request object is like a detailed package delivered to your doorstep. It contains all the information about the incoming request, such as:

- **Method:** Tells you what the client wants to do (e.g., GET to retrieve data, POST to submit data).
- **URL:** The address the client requested (e.g., /products/123).
- **Headers:** Metadata about the request, like the client's browser, accepted languages, and cookies.
- **Body:** Any data the client sent with the request, like form data or a JSON payload.

You can access this information using various methods provided by the http.Request object. For example:

- r.Method: Gets the HTTP method (e.g., "GET", "POST").
- r.URL.Path: Gets the path part of the URL (e.g., "/products/123").
- r.Header.Get("User-Agent"): Gets the value of the "User-Agent" header.
- r.Body: Gets the request body as an io.ReadCloser.

2. http.ResponseWriter

The http.ResponseWriter object is your tool for constructing and sending the HTTP response back to the client. It's like a blank canvas where you paint the response with the appropriate data and instructions.

Here are some key methods you can use with http.ResponseWriter:

- w.Header().Set("Content-Type", "application/json"): Sets the "Content-Type" header to indicate the type of data in the response (e.g., JSON, HTML).
- w.WriteHeader(http.StatusOK): Sets the HTTP status code of the response (e.g., 200 OK, 404 Not Found).
- fmt.Fprintln(w, "Hello!"): Writes data to the response body.

A Complete Handler Function

Let's see a complete example of a handler function that receives a request, processes it, and sends back a JSON response:

Go

```go
package main

import (

    "encoding/json"

    "fmt"

    "net/http"

)

type Product struct {

    ID      int     `json:"id"`

    Name    string `json:"name"`

    Price float64 `json:"price"`

}

func productHandler(w http.ResponseWriter, r *http.Request) {

    if r.Method == http.MethodGet {

        // Logic to fetch product from a database based on the request (e.g., from URL parameters)
```

```go
        product := Product{ID: 123, Name:
"Laptop", Price: 999.99} // Replace with actual
product data

        w.Header().Set("Content-Type",
"application/json")

        json.NewEncoder(w).Encode(product)

    } else if r.Method == http.MethodPost {

        // Logic to decode JSON request body
and create a new product in the database

        w.WriteHeader(http.StatusCreated) //
Send 201 Created status code

    } else {

        http.Error(w, "Invalid request method",
http.StatusMethodNotAllowed)

    }

}

func main() {

    http.HandleFunc("/products", productHandler)

    fmt.Println("Server listening on port 8080")

    http.ListenAndServe(":8080", nil)

}
```

In this code:

- We define a productHandler function that handles requests to /products.
- We check the r.Method to determine if it's a GET or POST request.
- For GET requests, we fetch the product data (simulated here) and send it back as a JSON response.
- For POST requests, we would decode the request body, create a new product, and send a 201 Created status code.
- For any other request method, we send a 405 Method Not Allowed error.

Real-World Examples

- User Authentication: When you log in to a website, your browser sends a POST request with your username and password. The server checks your credentials and sends back a response indicating success or failure.
- File Uploads: When you upload a file, your browser sends a POST request with the file data in the request body. The server receives the file, processes it (e.g., stores it, analyzes it), and sends back a response.
- API Calls: When a mobile app fetches data from a server, it sends a GET request. The server retrieves the data (e.g., from a database) and sends it back as a JSON response, which the app then uses to display information to the user.

By understanding how to handle HTTP requests and responses in Go, you gain the ability to build dynamic and interactive web applications that can communicate with clients, process data, and provide meaningful results. This is a fundamental skill for any backend developer, and you'll continue to build upon it as you progress through this book.

2.4 Routing and Middleware

As you build more complex web applications with Go, you'll often need to handle requests to different URLs and perform various actions based on the requested path. This is where routing comes into play. Routing is like a traffic controller within your application, directing incoming requests to the appropriate handler functions based on the requested URL.

Basic Routing with net/http

Go's net/http package provides a simple way to handle routing with the http.HandleFunc function. This function allows you to map URL paths to specific handler functions.[1]

For example, let's say you want to handle requests to the following URLs:

- /: Display the homepage.
- /about: Display the about page.
- /contact: Display the contact page.

You could use http.HandleFunc like this:

```Go
package main

import (

    "fmt"

    "net/http"

)

func homeHandler(w http.ResponseWriter, r *http.Request) {
```

```go
        fmt.Fprintln(w, "Welcome to the homepage!")

}

func aboutHandler(w http.ResponseWriter, r
*http.Request) {

        fmt.Fprintln(w, "This is the about page.")

}

func contactHandler(w http.ResponseWriter, r
*http.Request) {

        fmt.Fprintln(w, "Contact us at
support@example.com")

}

func main() {

        http.HandleFunc("/", homeHandler)

        http.HandleFunc("/about", aboutHandler)

        http.HandleFunc("/contact", contactHandler)

        fmt.Println("Server listening on port 8080")

        http.ListenAndServe(":8080", nil)

}
```

In this code, we define three handler functions (homeHandler, aboutHandler, contactHandler) and use http.HandleFunc to map them to their respective URL paths. When a request comes in for /, the homeHandler is executed, and so on.

Advanced Routing with Gorilla Mux

While http.HandleFunc is sufficient for basic routing, you might need more advanced features as your application grows. This is where third-party routing libraries like Gorilla Mux come in handy.

Gorilla Mux provides a more flexible and powerful way to handle routing in Go.[2] Here are some of its key features:

- Variable Paths: Define routes with variables to capture dynamic parts of the URL. For example, /users/{id} can match /users/123, /users/456, etc., and you can access the value of {id} in your handler function.
- Path Patterns: Match routes based on regular expressions for more complex patterns.[3] For example, you could define a route that matches any URL starting with /products/.
- Subrouters: Create sub routers to organize your routes into logical groups. This can be helpful for larger applications with many endpoints.

Here's an example of using Gorilla Mux to define routes with variables:

```Go
package main

import (

    "fmt"

    "net/http"

    "github.com/gorilla/mux"

)
```

```go
func userHandler(w http.ResponseWriter, r
*http.Request) {

    vars := mux.Vars(r)

    userID := vars["id"]

    fmt.Fprintf(w, "Retrieving user with ID:
%s\n", userID)

}

func main() {

    router := mux.NewRouter()

    router.HandleFunc("/users/{id}",
userHandler)

    fmt.Println("Server listening on port 8080")

    http.ListenAndServe(":8080", router)

}
```

In this code, we use mux.NewRouter() to create a new router. Then, we use router.HandleFunc("/users/{id}", userHandler) to define a route with a variable named id. In the userHandler function, we use mux.Vars(r) to access the route variables and retrieve the value of id.

Middleware

Middleware functions act as intermediaries between the client request and the final handler function. They allow you to add common functionality across multiple routes without repeating code.

Think of middleware like a series of checkpoints that a request passes through before reaching its destination. Each checkpoint can perform a specific action, such as:

- Authentication: Verify the user's identity before allowing access to protected resources.
- Logging: Log request details for debugging and monitoring.
- Request Validation: Ensure the request has the required data and format.
- Error Handling: Catch and handle errors gracefully.

Here's an example of a simple middleware function that logs the request method and URL:

```Go
package main

import (

    "fmt"

    "log"

    "net/http"

)

func loggingMiddleware(next http.Handler)
http.Handler {

    return http.HandlerFunc(func(w
http.ResponseWriter, r *http.Request) {

        log.Printf("Request: %s %s", r.Method,
r.URL.Path)

        next.ServeHTTP(w, r) // Call the next
handler in the chain
```

```go
    })

}

func handler(w http.ResponseWriter, r
*http.Request) {

    fmt.Fprintln(w, "Hello from the handler!")

}

func main() {

    // Wrap the handler with the logging
middleware

    http.Handle("/",
loggingMiddleware(http.HandlerFunc(handler)))

    fmt.Println("Server listening on port 8080")

    http.ListenAndServe(":8080", nil)

}
```

In this code, loggingMiddleware takes the next handler in the chain as an argument and returns a new handler. This new handler logs the request details and then calls the next handler using next.ServeHTTP(w, r). This way, the request passes through the logging middleware before reaching the final handler.

Real-World Examples

Routing and middleware are essential components of many web applications:

- REST APIs: Routing is used to define different endpoints for accessing resources, and middleware can be used for authentication, authorization, and rate limiting.

- Single-Page Applications (SPAs): Routing can be used to handle different views within a SPA, and middleware can be used for tasks like data fetching and state management.[4]
- Content Management Systems (CMS): Routing is used to display different pages and content based on the URL, and middleware can be used for tasks like caching and security.

2.5 Working with JSON and Data Serialization

In web development, data is constantly flowing between clients (like web browsers or mobile apps) and servers. To ensure this data can be understood and processed by both sides, we need a common language – a standardized format for representing and exchanging information. This is where JSON (JavaScript Object Notation) comes in.

JSON is a lightweight, text-based data format that has become the de facto standard for web APIs. It's human-readable, easy to parse, and supported by a wide range of programming languages, including Go.

JSON is a way to represent data structures like objects and arrays in a textual form. It uses a simple syntax based on key-value pairs and lists. Here's a quick example of JSON data:

JSON

```
{

  "name": "Alice",

  "age": 30,

  "email": "alice@example.com",

  "address": {
```

```
    "street": "123 Main St",

    "city": "Anytown",

    "country": "USA"

  },

  "interests": ["reading", "coding", "hiking"]

}
```

In this example, we have a JSON object that represents a person. It contains key-value pairs, where the keys are strings (like "name", "age", "email") and the values can be different data types (strings, numbers, booleans, other objects, or arrays).

Serialization and Deserialization

To use JSON in your Go applications, you need to understand two key processes:

- Serialization: This is the process of converting Go data structures (like structs or maps) into JSON format. It's like packaging your data into a format that can be easily transmitted over a network or stored in a file.
- Deserialization: This is the reverse process – converting JSON data back into Go data structures. It's like unpacking the data received from a client or read from a file.

Go's encoding/json Package

Go provides a powerful package called encoding/json that makes working with JSON a breeze. This package offers functions for both serialization and deserialization.

- **json.Marshal(...):** This function takes a Go data structure (like a struct) and converts it into a JSON-formatted byte slice.
- **json.Unmarshal(...):** This function takes a JSON-formatted byte slice and converts it into a Go data structure.

Code Example: Serializing and Deserializing a Struct

Let's see a practical example of how to use encoding/json to serialize and deserialize a Go struct:

```go
Go

package main

import (

    "encoding/json"

    "fmt"

)

type User struct {

    Name    string `json:"name"`

    Age     int     `json:"age"`

    Email string `json:"email"`

}

func main() {

    // Create a User struct

    user := User{Name: "Alice", Age: 30, Email:
"alice@example.com"}
```

```go
    // Serialize the User struct to JSON

    jsonData, err := json.Marshal(user)

    if err != nil {

        fmt.Println("Error serializing JSON:",
err)

        return

    }

    fmt.Println(string(jsonData)) // Output:
{"name":"Alice","age":30,"email":"alice@example.c
om"}

    // Deserialize the JSON data back into a
User struct

    var decodedUser User

    err = json.Unmarshal(jsonData, &decodedUser)

    if err != nil {

        fmt.Println("Error deserializing
JSON:", err)

        return

    }

    fmt.Println(decodedUser) // Output: {Alice
30 alice@example.com}

}
```

In this code:

- We define a User struct with fields for name, age, and email.
- We create a User object and serialize it to JSON using json.Marshal.
- We then deserialize the JSON data back into a User object using json.Unmarshal.

Working with JSON in HTTP Requests and Responses

In web applications, you often need to send and receive JSON data in HTTP requests and responses. Here's how you can do that in Go:

- Sending JSON Responses: To send a JSON response, you set the Content-Type header to application/json and use json.NewEncoder(w).Encode(data) to write the JSON data to the response writer.
- Receiving JSON Requests: To receive JSON data in a request body, you use json.NewDecoder(r.Body).Decode(&data) to decode the JSON data into a Go data structure.

Real-World Examples

JSON is used extensively in various web applications:

- REST APIs: JSON is the most common format for exchanging data between clients and servers in RESTful APIs.
- Single-Page Applications (SPAs): SPAs often rely on JSON to fetch data from servers and update the user interface dynamically.
- Mobile Apps: Mobile apps frequently use JSON to communicate with backend servers and exchange data.
- Configuration Files: JSON is often used to store configuration settings in a human-readable format.

Chapter 3: Interacting with Databases

Databases are like organized storage systems for your application's data. They allow you to store, retrieve, and manage data efficiently and reliably. In this chapter, we'll explore how to interact with different types of databases using Go, focusing on both SQL and NoSQL databases.

3.1 Connecting to SQL Databases

SQL databases. SQL stands for Structured Query Language, and it's the standard way to interact with relational databases. These databases are like well-organized spreadsheets, with data neatly arranged in rows and columns within tables. They excel at storing structured data and managing relationships between different pieces of information.

Think of an online store, for example. You might have a products table to store product information (name, description, price), a customers table for customer details, and an orders table to track orders. Each order in the orders table would be linked to a customer in the customers table and one or more products in the products table. This interconnectedness is what makes SQL databases so powerful for managing complex data relationships.

Two of the most popular SQL databases are PostgreSQL and MySQL. They are both open-source, robust, and widely used in various applications. Let's walk through how you can connect to them from your Go programs.

1. Install the Database Driver

Before you can connect to a database, you need the right driver – a piece of software that acts as a bridge between your Go application and the database. Think of it as a translator that allows your Go code to communicate with the database in a language they both understand.

You can use the go get command to install the necessary drivers:

- For PostgreSQL: go get github.com/lib/pq
- For MySQL: go get github.com/go-sql-driver/mysql

This command downloads and installs the driver package, making it available for your Go projects.

2. Import the database/sql **Package**

Go's standard library provides a powerful package called database/sql. This package offers a generic interface for interacting with SQL databases, regardless of the specific database system you're using (PostgreSQL, MySQL, or others).

To use this package, import it into your Go file:

```Go
import "database/sql"
```

This line brings in the database/sql package, giving you access to its functions and types for working with databases.

3. Connect to the Database

Now, let's establish a connection to your database. You'll use the sql.Open() function, which takes two arguments:

- Driver Name: A string that identifies the database driver you're using (e.g., "postgres" for PostgreSQL, "mysql" for MySQL).
- Connection String: A string that provides the necessary details to connect to your database, such as the username, password, host, port, and database name.

Here's an example of how to connect to a MySQL database:

```go
Go

package main

import (

    "database/sql"

    "fmt"

    "log"

    _ "github.com/go-sql-driver/mysql" // Import
the MySQL driver

)

func main() {

    // Construct the connection string

    dbUser := "your_db_user"

    dbPass := "your_db_password"

    dbName := "your_db_name"

    dbHost := "localhost"

    dbPort := "3306"

    connectionString :=
fmt.Sprintf("%s:%s@tcp(%s:%s)/%s", dbUser,
dbPass, dbHost, dbPort, dbName)

    // Open a connection to the database
```

```
    db, err := sql.Open("mysql",
connectionString)

    if err != nil {

        log.Fatal(err) // Handle the error
appropriately (e.g., log it, return an error)

    }

    defer db.Close() // Close the connection
when the function exits

    // ... use the db object to interact with
the database ...

}
```

In this code:

- We import the MySQL driver. The underscore (_) before
  "github.com/go-sql-driver/mysql" indicates that we're
  importing the package for its side effects (initializing the
  driver) and not directly using its exported identifiers.
- We construct the connection string using the database
  credentials.
- We use sql.Open("mysql", connectionString) to create a
  database connection.
- We use defer db.Close() to ensure that the database
  connection is closed when the function exits, preventing
  resource leaks.

Always handle potential errors when connecting to a database. In
this example, we use log.Fatal(err) to log the error and exit the
program if the connection fails. In a real-world application, you
might want to handle errors more gracefully, such as returning an
error message or retrying the connection.

4. A Word About Connection Strings

Connection strings can vary slightly depending on the database system you're using. Here are some general guidelines:

- PostgreSQL: A typical PostgreSQL connection string might look like this: "postgres://username:password@host:port/dbname"
- MySQL: A common MySQL connection string might look like this: "username:password@tcp(host:port)/dbname"

You can find more specific connection string formats in the documentation for your database driver.

Real-World Example: Connecting to a Production Database

In a real-world scenario, you'll likely store your database credentials in environment variables or a configuration file rather than hardcoding them directly in your code. This is a good security practice and makes it easier to manage your application across different environments (development, staging, production).

For example, you might retrieve the database credentials from environment variables like this:

```Go
dbUser := os.Getenv("DB_USER")

dbPass := os.Getenv("DB_PASSWORD")

// ... and so on ...
```

This allows you to configure different database credentials for different environments without modifying your code.

By following these steps, you can successfully connect your Go applications to PostgreSQL and MySQL databases. This opens up a world of possibilities for storing, retrieving, and managing data in your applications. In the next section, we'll explore how to execute queries and interact with the data in your database.

3.2 Using Go with NoSQL Databases

Let's discuss a different approach to data storage: NoSQL databases. While SQL databases are excellent for structured data and relationships, NoSQL databases offer more flexibility and scalability, especially for applications with evolving data structures or massive amounts of unstructured data.

Think of a social media platform where users can post different types of content — text, images, videos, links, etc. Trying to fit all this diverse data into a rigid SQL schema with rows and columns can be challenging. This is where NoSQL databases shine. They allow you to store data in more flexible formats, adapting to the ever-changing needs of your application.

One of the most popular NoSQL databases is MongoDB. It uses a document-oriented model, where data is stored in JSON-like documents. These documents can have varying structures, allowing you to store different types of information within the same collection.

1. Install the MongoDB Driver

Just as with SQL databases, you need a driver to connect your Go application to MongoDB. You can use the go get command to install the official MongoDB driver for Go:

```Bash
go get go.mongodb.org/mongo-driver/mongo
```

This command downloads and installs the necessary packages to interact with MongoDB.

2. Connect to MongoDB

To connect to your MongoDB server, you'll use the mongo.Connect() function. This function takes context and client options as arguments. The context provides a way to manage deadlines and cancellations for the connection operation, while the client options allow you to configure various connection parameters.

Here's an example of how to connect to a MongoDB server running on your local machine:

```Go
package main

import (

    "context"

    "fmt"

    "log"

    "go.mongodb.org/mongo-driver/mongo"

    "go.mongodb.org/mongo-driver/mongo/options"

)

func main() {

    // Construct the connection URI

    uri := "mongodb://localhost:27017" //
Replace with your actual MongoDB URI

    // Create client options
```

```go
    clientOptions :=
options.Client().ApplyURI(uri)

    // Connect to MongoDB

    client, err :=
mongo.Connect(context.Background(),
clientOptions)

    if err != nil {

        log.Fatal(err)

    }

    defer
client.Disconnect(context.Background()) // Close
the connection when the function exits

    // ... use the client object to interact
with the database ...

}
```

In this code:

- We create a clientOptions object with the MongoDB connection URI.
- We use mongo.Connect() with the background context and client options to establish a connection to the MongoDB server.
- We use defer client.Disconnect() to ensure that the connection is closed when the function exits.

3. Access Databases and Collections

Once you have a MongoDB client, you can access databases and collections within that server.

- Databases: A MongoDB server can host multiple databases. You can access a specific database using the client.Database("database_name") method.
- Collections: Within a database, you have collections, which are like tables in SQL databases. You can access a collection using the database.Collection("collection_name") method.

4. Working with Documents

In MongoDB, data is stored in documents, which are JSON-like structures. You can use the bson.M type to represent documents in Go.

Here's an example of how to insert, find, and update documents in a MongoDB collection:

```Go
package main

import (

    "context"

    "fmt"

    "log"

    "go.mongodb.org/mongo-driver/bson"

    "go.mongodb.org/mongo-driver/mongo"

    "go.mongodb.org/mongo-driver/mongo/options"

)

func main() {
```

```go
// ... (Connect to MongoDB as shown in the
previous example) ...

// Get a handle to the "users" collection in
the "test" database

collection :=
client.Database("test").Collection("users")

// Insert a document

user := bson.M{"name": "Alice", "email":
"alice@example.com"}

result, err :=
collection.InsertOne(context.Background(), user)

if err != nil {

    log.Fatal(err)

}

fmt.Println("Inserted document ID:",
result.InsertedID)

// Find a document

filter := bson.M{"name": "Alice"}

var foundUser bson.M

err =
collection.FindOne(context.Background(),
filter).Decode(&foundUser)

if err != nil {

    log.Fatal(err)
```

```go
    }

    fmt.Println("Found user:", foundUser)

    // Update a document

    update := bson.M{"$set": bson.M{"age": 30}}

    _, err =
collection.UpdateOne(context.Background(),
filter, update)

    if err != nil {

        log.Fatal(err)

    }

    fmt.Println("Updated user age")

}
```

In this code:

- We get a handle to the "users" collection in the "test" database.
- We insert a new document representing a user.
- We use a filter to find a document with the name "Alice".
- We update the "age" field of the found document.

Real-World Examples

MongoDB is used in a wide range of applications:

- Content Management Systems: Storing articles, blog posts, and other content with varying structures.
- E-commerce Platforms: Managing product catalogs, user profiles, and shopping carts.

- Social Media Platforms: Storing user data, posts, comments, and activity feeds.
- Real-time Analytics: Analyzing large volumes of data generated by sensors, applications, and user interactions.

By understanding how to use Go with MongoDB, you gain the ability to leverage the flexibility and scalability of NoSQL databases for your applications. This opens up new possibilities for managing data and building applications that can adapt to evolving needs.

3.3 Object-Relational Mapping with GORM

While interacting with databases directly using SQL queries is powerful, it can sometimes feel a bit cumbersome. You have to write raw SQL statements, worry about escaping values correctly to prevent SQL injection vulnerabilities, and manually map query results to your Go data structures.

Object-Relational Mapping (ORM) offers a more convenient and developer-friendly approach. They act as a bridge between your Go code and the database, allowing you to interact with the database using Go objects and methods instead of raw SQL. It's like having a translator that seamlessly converts your Go code into the language the database understands.

One of the most popular ORM libraries for Go is GORM. It provides a clean and expressive way to interact with various SQL databases, including PostgreSQL, MySQL, SQLite, and more. GORM takes care of the underlying SQL queries, allowing you to focus on your application logic.

1. Install GORM

Before you can use GORM, you need to install it. You can use the go get command to install both GORM and the database driver for your chosen database:

Bash

```
go get gorm.io/gorm

go get gorm.io/driver/mysql // Or any other
database driver you need (e.g., postgres, sqlite)
```

This command downloads and installs the necessary GORM packages and the specific database driver you'll be using.

2. Define Your Models

In GORM, you define your data structures as Go structs. These structs represent the tables in your database, and the struct fields represent the columns. GORM provides some handy tags that you can use to customize how your structs are mapped to the database.

Here's an example of a User struct that you might use to represent a users table:

Go

```
type User struct {

  gorm.Model  // Includes ID, CreatedAt,
UpdatedAt, DeletedAt

  Name   string

  Email  string `gorm:"uniqueIndex"`

  Age    uint

}
```

In this code:

- We embed gorm.Model to include common fields like ID, CreatedAt, UpdatedAt, and DeletedAt.
- We use the gorm:"uniqueIndex" tag to create a unique index on the Email field, ensuring that no two users have the same email address.

3. Connect to the Database and AutoMigrate

To start using GORM, you need to connect to your database and let GORM know about your models. GORM's Open() function establishes a connection to the database, and the AutoMigrate() function automatically creates the necessary tables based on your models.

Go

```go
package main

import (

    "fmt"

    "log"

    "gorm.io/driver/mysql"

    "gorm.io/gorm"

)

func main() {

    // Construct the connection string

    dsn :=
"user:password@tcp(127.0.0.1:3306)/dbname?charset
=utf8mb4&parseTime=True&loc=Local"
```

```go
    // Connect to the database

    db, err := gorm.Open(mysql.Open(dsn),
&gorm.Config{})

    if err != nil {

        log.Fatal(err)

    }

    // AutoMigrate the User model

    db.AutoMigrate(&User{})

    // ... use the db object to interact with
the database ...

}
```

In this code:

- We construct the connection string for our MySQL database.
- We use gorm.Open() to create a GORM database instance.
- We call db.AutoMigrate(&User{}) to create the users table (if it doesn't exist) based on the User model.

4. Perform CRUD Operations

Once you have a GORM database instance, you can use its methods to perform CRUD (Create, Read, Update, Delete) operations on your models.

- **Create:**

Go

```
user := User{Name: "Alice", Email:
"alice@example.com", Age: 30}

db.Create(&user)
```

- **Read:**

```Go
var user User

db.First(&user, 1) // Find user with ID 1
```

- **Update:**

```Go
db.Model(&user).Update("Name", "Alicia")
```

- **Delete:**

```Go
db.Delete(&user)
```

GORM provides a wide range of methods for querying, filtering, and ordering data. You can find detailed documentation and examples on the official GORM website.

Real-World Examples

GORM is used in various Go applications to simplify database interactions:

- Web Applications: Building REST APIs that interact with a database to store and retrieve user data, product information, or other application data.
- Content Management Systems: Managing content, users, and settings stored in a database.
- E-commerce Platforms: Handling product catalogs, orders, and customer information.

Benefits of Using GORM

- Increased Productivity: GORM reduces the amount of boilerplate code you need to write for database interactions, allowing you to focus on your application logic.
- Improved Code Readability: GORM's syntax is more expressive and easier to read than raw SQL queries.
- Reduced Errors: GORM helps prevent common database errors like SQL injection vulnerabilities by automatically escaping values.
- Database Agnostic: GORM supports multiple database systems, making it easier to switch databases if needed.

3.4 Database Best Practices

When working with databases in your Go applications, it's important to follow best practices to ensure data integrity, performance, and efficiency. Let's discuss two essential concepts that can significantly improve your database interactions: transactions and connection pooling.

Transactions

Think of a database transaction as a safety net for your data. It allows you to group multiple database operations into a single unit of work. This means that either all the operations within a transaction succeed, or none of them do. This ensures that your data remains consistent and avoids partial updates that could lead to inconsistencies or errors.

Let's say you're building a banking application, and you need to transfer money from one account to another. This involves two operations: deducting the amount from the sender's account and adding it to the recipient's account. If one of these operations fails while the other succeeds, you'll end up with an inconsistent state – money might disappear or appear out of thin air!

Transactions prevent this by ensuring that both operations are executed as an atomic unit. If either operation fails, the entire transaction is rolled back, and the database remains in its original state.

Here's how you can use transactions in Go with the database/sql package:

```Go
package main

import (

    "database/sql"

    "fmt"

    "log"

)

func transferMoney(db *sql.DB, fromAccountID int, toAccountID int, amount float64) error {

    // Begin a transaction

    tx, err := db.Begin()
```

```go
        if err != nil {

            return err

        }

        defer func() {

            if p := recover(); p != nil {

                tx.Rollback()

                panic(p) // re-throw panic after
Rollback

            } else if err != nil {

                tx.Rollback() // err is non-nil;
don't change it

            } else {

                err = tx.Commit() // err is nil;
if Commit returns error update err

            }

        }()

        // Deduct from the sender's account

        _, err = tx.Exec("UPDATE accounts SET
balance = balance - ? WHERE id = ?", amount,
fromAccountID)

        if err != nil {

            return err

        }
```

```go
    // Add to the recipient's account

    _, err = tx.Exec("UPDATE accounts SET
balance = balance + ? WHERE id = ?", amount,
toAccountID)

    if err != nil {

        return err

    }

    return nil // Transaction will be committed
if no errors occurred

}

func main() {

    // ... (Connect to the database) ...

    err := transferMoney(db, 1, 2, 100.00)

    if err != nil {

        log.Fatal(err)

    }

    fmt.Println("Money transferred
successfully")

}
```

In this code:

- We use db.Begin() to start a transaction.
- We execute the SQL queries to update the account balances within the transaction.

- If any error occurs during the transaction, we call tx.Rollback() to undo the changes.
- If all operations succeed, we call tx.Commit() to commit the changes to the database.

Connection Pooling

Opening and closing a new database connection for every query can be an expensive operation. It involves network communication, authentication, and resource allocation. Connection pooling helps optimize this process by maintaining a pool of open connections that can be reused for multiple queries.

Think of it like a car rental service. Instead of buying a new car every time you need to go somewhere, you rent a car from a pool of available vehicles. When you're done, you return the car to the pool for someone else to use.

Connection pooling provides several benefits:

- Reduced Overhead: Reusing existing connections eliminates the overhead of establishing new connections for each query.
- Improved Performance: Faster query execution due to readily available connections.
- Resource Efficiency: Limits the number of open connections, preventing resource exhaustion on the database server.

You can configure connection pooling parameters using the db.SetMaxIdleConns() and db.SetMaxOpenConns() methods in the database/sql package.

```Go
db.SetMaxIdleConns(10)  // Set the maximum number
of idle connections in the pool
```

```
db.SetMaxOpenConns(100) // Set the maximum number
of open connections to the database
```

Real-World Examples

Transactions and connection pooling are crucial for building robust and efficient database interactions in real-world applications:

- E-commerce Platforms: Transactions ensure that order processing and inventory updates are handled consistently. Connection pooling improves the performance of product searches and checkout processes.
- Financial Applications: Transactions are essential for maintaining the integrity of financial data, such as account balances and transactions. Connection pooling ensures efficient access to account information and transaction history.
- Social Media Platforms: Transactions can be used to handle user interactions, such as posting comments or liking posts, in a consistent manner. Connection pooling ensures that the platform can handle a large number of concurrent users.

By understanding and applying these database best practices, you can ensure that your Go applications interact with databases effectively, maintaining data integrity and optimizing performance.

Chapter 4: Microservices Architecture with Go

You've mastered the basics of Go and database interactions. Now, let's step into modern software architecture: microservices. This architectural style has taken the software development world by storm, offering a way to build more flexible, scalable, and maintainable applications. And guess what? Go is a fantastic language for building microservices!

4.1 Understanding Microservices

Think of a large, complex system like a car. Instead of building it as one giant, inseparable piece, you design it as a collection of smaller, independent components – the engine, the transmission, the brakes, the electrical system, and so on. Each component has a specific function and can be developed, tested, and replaced independently without affecting the other parts.

Microservices architecture applies this same principle to software development. Instead of building a monolithic application where all the functionality is tightly interwoven, you break it down into smaller, self-contained services. Each service focuses on a specific business capability and communicates with other services through well-defined[1] APIs (Application Programming Interfaces).[2]

For instance, consider an e-commerce platform. In a microservices architecture, you might have separate services for:

- Product Catalog Service: Manages product information, inventory, search functionality, and product recommendations.
- Order Management Service: Handles order creation, payment processing, shipping, and order tracking.
- User Accounts Service: Manages user registration, login, profiles, and authentication.

- Shopping Cart Service: Allows users to add and remove items from their shopping carts and manage their shopping sessions.
- Notification Service: Sends notifications to users about order updates, promotions, or other relevant events.

Each of these services operates independently, has its own database, and can be developed, deployed, and scaled without affecting the others. This modularity provides numerous benefits.

Benefits of Microservices Architecture

- Improved Agility and Faster Development: Smaller services are easier to develop, test, and deploy. Teams can work on different services concurrently, allowing for faster development cycles and more frequent releases. This agility is crucial in today's fast-paced software development environment.
- Increased Scalability: Each service can be scaled independently based on its specific needs. This allows you to allocate resources more efficiently and handle varying workloads without over-provisioning resources for the entire application. For example, if your product catalog service experiences a surge in traffic during a sale, you can scale it up without affecting other services.
- Enhanced Resilience and Fault Isolation: If one service experiences an error or failure, it doesn't necessarily bring down the entire application. Other services can continue to function, providing a more robust and resilient system. This fault isolation is crucial for applications that require high availability.
- Technology Diversity: Microservices architecture gives you the freedom to choose different technologies and programming languages for different services. This allows you to select the best tool for the job and avoid being locked into a single technology stack. For example, you might use Go for a performance-critical service, Python for a machine

learning service, and Node.js for a real-time communication service.

- Easier Maintenance and Updates: Smaller codebases are easier to understand, maintain, and update. This reduces the risk of introducing bugs or regressions when making changes. When you need to update a specific functionality, you only need to modify the relevant service, leaving other services untouched.
- Reusability: Well-designed microservices can be reused across different applications or projects, promoting efficiency and consistency. For example, a user accounts service could be reused across multiple applications within your organization.

Principles of Microservices

To effectively implement a microservices architecture, it's essential to adhere to certain principles:

- Single Responsibility: Each service should have a single, well-defined responsibility. This promotes modularity and makes services easier to understand and manage.
- Loose Coupling: Services should be loosely coupled, meaning they should have minimal dependencies on each other. This allows services to evolve independently and reduces the impact of changes in one service on others.
- Independent Deployment: Each service should be independently deployable. This allows for faster and more frequent releases without affecting other parts of the system.
- Decentralized Governance: Teams should have autonomy in choosing the technologies and tools they use to build and deploy their services. This promotes innovation and allows teams to select the best solutions for their specific needs.

Real-World Examples

Many successful companies have adopted microservices architecture to build and scale their applications:

- Netflix: Netflix uses microservices to handle millions of concurrent users streaming video content. This allows them to scale different parts of their system independently, such as video encoding, recommendations, and user accounts.
- Amazon: Amazon has decomposed its massive e-commerce platform into thousands of microservices. This enables them to handle peak traffic during events like Black Friday and Prime Day, as well as continuously deploy new features and updates.
- Uber: Uber relies on microservices to manage various aspects of its ride-hailing service, including rider and driver matching, payment processing, and location tracking. This allows them to scale their services globally and adapt to different regional requirements.

4.2 Designing Microservices with Go

Now that you understand the principles and benefits of microservices, let's explore how to effectively design and build them using Go. Go's inherent features and ecosystem make it a compelling choice for crafting efficient and scalable microservices.

1. Define Service Boundaries

The first step in designing microservices is to determine the boundaries of each service. Each service should have a single, well-defined responsibility and focus on a specific business capability. This promotes modularity, making services easier to understand, develop, and maintain.

Think of an online store. You might have separate services for:

- Product Catalog Service: Manages product information, inventory, search functionality, and recommendations.

- Order Management Service: Handles order creation, payment processing, shipping, and order tracking.
- User Accounts Service: Manages user registration, login, profiles, and authentication.
- Payment Processing Service: Handles interactions with payment gateways to process transactions securely.

Each service encapsulates a specific domain and interacts with other services through well-defined APIs.

2. API Design

The way your services communicate with each other is crucial in a microservices architecture. APIs (Application Programming Interfaces) act as the communication channels between services. When designing APIs for your microservices, consider these factors:

- Clarity and Consistency: Use clear and consistent naming conventions, data formats, and error handling across your APIs. This makes it easier for different teams to understand and use your services.
- Versioning: As your services evolve, you'll likely need to make changes to your APIs. Implement versioning to allow clients to continue using older versions of your API while you introduce new versions with updated functionality.
- Documentation: Provide clear and comprehensive documentation for your APIs, including descriptions of endpoints, request and response formats, and error codes. This helps other developers understand and integrate with your services.

3. Data Management

In a microservices architecture, each service should ideally have its own dedicated database. This promotes loose coupling between services and prevents data dependencies that can make it difficult to modify or scale individual services.

Choose the right database technology for each service based on its specific needs. For example, you might use a relational database (like PostgreSQL or MySQL) for structured data in a product catalog service, a NoSQL database (like MongoDB) for flexible data in a user activity tracking service, and a key-value store (like Redis) for caching frequently accessed data.

4. Technology Choices

While Go is an excellent choice for building microservices, you have the flexibility to use other technologies for specific services if they better suit the needs of that service. For example, you might use Python for a machine learning service or Node.js for a real-time communication service.

However, be mindful of the operational overhead of managing multiple technologies. Strive for a balance between technology diversity and operational efficiency.

5. Error Handling and Logging

Robust error handling and logging are essential for microservices. Each service should handle errors gracefully, providing informative error messages and logging relevant information for debugging and monitoring.

Consider using centralized logging systems to aggregate logs from different services, making it easier to identify and troubleshoot issues in your application.

6. Observability

Observability is crucial for understanding the behavior and performance of your microservices. Implement monitoring, tracing, and metrics to gain insights into how your services are performing, identify bottlenecks, and detect anomalies.

Tools like Prometheus, Jaeger, and Grafana can help you collect and visualize metrics, traces, and logs from your services.

Code Example: A Simple Microservice in Go

Here's a basic example of a Go microservice that exposes a REST API for managing user accounts:

```Go
package main

import (

    "encoding/json"

    "fmt"

    "log"

    "net/http"

)

type User struct {

    ID      int      `json:"id"`

    Name    string   `json:"name"`

    Email   string   `json:"email"`

}

func getUsersHandler(w http.ResponseWriter, r *http.Request) {
```

```go
    // ... (Fetch users from the database) ...

    users := []User{

        {ID: 1, Name: "Alice", Email:
"alice@example.com"},

        {ID: 2, Name: "Bob", Email:
"bob@example.com"},

    }

    w.Header().Set("Content-Type",
"application/json")

    json.NewEncoder(w).Encode(users)

}

func main() {

    http.HandleFunc("/users", getUsersHandler)

    log.Println("User service listening on port
8080")

    log.Fatal(http.ListenAndServe(":8080", nil))

}
```

This code defines a simple HTTP server that responds to requests on the /users endpoint with a JSON representation of user data.

Real-World Examples

Many companies use Go to build microservices:

- Netflix: Uses Go for its server architecture to handle massive amounts of streaming data and ensure a smooth viewing experience.
- Uber: Utilizes Go for various services, including its geofence lookup microservice, which handles millions of requests per second.
- Dropbox: Migrated some of its performance-critical backend components from Python to Go, resulting in significant improvements in speed and efficiency.

4.3 Inter-service Communication

In a microservices architecture, your services need to talk to each other – exchange data, trigger actions, and collaborate to fulfill user requests.[1] This communication between services is crucial, and choosing the right approach can significantly impact your application's performance, scalability, and maintainability.[2]

Two popular approaches for inter-service communication are REST (Representational State Transfer) and gRPC (Google Remote Procedure Call). Let's explore each of them and understand their strengths and weaknesses.

REST (Representational State Transfer)

REST is a widely adopted architectural style for building web APIs.[3] It leverages the principles of HTTP – the same protocol that powers the web – to create APIs that are easy to understand, use, and integrate with.[4]

Here's how REST typically works for inter-service communication:

- Resources: Services expose resources, which can be any piece of data or functionality that other services might need to access.[5] These resources are identified by unique URLs (Uniform Resource Locators).[6]

- HTTP Methods: Services use standard HTTP methods (GET, POST, PUT, DELETE) to interact with these resources.[7] For example, a GET request might retrieve data, a POST request might create a new resource, and so on.
- Data Format: JSON (JavaScript Object Notation) is the most common data format used in RESTful APIs. It's a human-readable, text-based format that's easy to parse and generate.[8]

Example:

Let's say you have an e-commerce application with a Product Catalog Service and an Order Management Service. The Order Management Service might use a REST API to communicate with the Product Catalog Service to:

- Get product details: Send a GET request to /products/{id} to retrieve information about a specific product.
- Update product inventory: Send a PUT request to /products/{id} to update the stock quantity of a product after an order is placed.

Advantages of REST:

- Simplicity and Familiarity: REST leverages familiar HTTP concepts, making it easy to understand and use.[9]
- Wide Adoption: REST is widely adopted, with numerous tools and libraries available for various programming languages and platforms.[10]
- Flexibility: REST allows for flexibility in data formats and communication patterns.[11]

Disadvantages of REST:

- Performance Overhead: JSON serialization and deserialization can introduce performance overhead, especially for large datasets or frequent communication.[12]
- Over-fetching: Clients often receive more data than they need, as REST APIs typically return fixed data structures.
- Coupling: REST APIs can sometimes create coupling between services, as clients need to know the specific URLs and data formats used by the server.

gRPC (Google Remote Procedure Call)

gRPC is a modern, high-performance framework for remote procedure calls.[13] It offers a more efficient and streamlined approach to inter-service communication, especially for internal communication within a microservices architecture.

Here's how gRPC works:

- Protocol Buffers: gRPC uses Protocol Buffers (protobuf), a language-agnostic mechanism for serializing structured data.[14] Protobuf is more compact and efficient than JSON, resulting in faster serialization and deserialization.[15]
- Contract-First Approach: gRPC uses a contract-first approach, where you define the service interface and data structures in a protobuf file.[16] This file is then used to generate code for both the client and the server in various programming languages.[17]
- Streaming: gRPC supports streaming, allowing services to send and receive a stream of messages, which is useful for scenarios like real-time updates or large data transfers.[18]

Example:

In the same e-commerce application, the Order Management Service could use gRPC to communicate with the Product Catalog Service:

- Get product details: Make a gRPC call to the GetProductDetails method, passing the product ID as an argument.
- Update product inventory: Make a gRPC call to the UpdateInventory method, passing the product ID and the quantity change as arguments.

Advantages of gRPC:

- Performance: Protobuf's efficient encoding and gRPC's optimized communication protocol result in significantly faster communication compared to REST.[19]
- Type Safety: The contract-first approach with protobuf ensures type safety and reduces errors due to data type mismatches.[20]
- Streaming: gRPC's support for streaming enables efficient handling of real-time updates and large data transfers.[21]

Disadvantages of gRPC:

- Less Browser-Friendly: gRPC is not as directly compatible with web browsers as REST, requiring proxies or gateways for browser-based communication.
- Steeper Learning Curve: gRPC has a slightly steeper learning curve compared to REST, as it involves learning protobuf and the gRPC framework.[22]

Choosing Between REST and gRPC

The choice between REST and gRPC depends on your specific needs and constraints:

- External APIs: For external-facing APIs or when interoperability with different systems is crucial, REST is often the preferred choice due to its wide adoption and simplicity.

- Internal Communication: For internal communication between microservices where performance and efficiency are paramount, gRPC is a strong contender.
- Real-time Updates: If your application requires real-time updates or streaming data, gRPC's streaming capabilities make it a good fit.[23]
- Browser Support: If you need direct communication between your microservices and web browsers, REST is generally more straightforward.

4.4 Service Discovery and Load Balancing

In a microservices architecture, your services are often deployed across multiple instances and potentially across different machines or even data centers. This distributed nature brings challenges: How do services find each other? How do you distribute traffic effectively among those instances?

This is where service discovery and load balancing come into play. These crucial components help manage the dynamic nature of microservices and ensure that your application remains scalable, reliable, and performant.

Service Discovery

Think of service discovery as a dynamic phone book for your microservices. In a traditional setup, you might hardcode the addresses of your services in your code. But in a microservices world where services can be deployed and scaled dynamically, hardcoding addresses is not feasible.

Service discovery provides a mechanism for services to register themselves and discover other services in the system. It's like each service has its own entry in the phone book, and other services can look them up by name to find their current location (IP address and port).

Here's how service discovery typically works:

1. Registration: When a service instance starts up, it registers itself with the service discovery system, providing its name, address, and other relevant information.
2. Discovery: When a service needs to communicate with another service, it queries the service discovery system to find the available instances of that service.
3. Health Checks: The service discovery system often performs health checks on registered services to ensure they are alive and responding. If a service instance fails, it's removed from the registry.

Benefits of Service Discovery:

- Dynamic Updates: Services can be added, removed, or relocated without requiring manual configuration changes.
- Resilience: If a service instance fails, other instances can be automatically discovered, ensuring continuous operation.
- Simplified Configuration: Services don't need to know the specific addresses of other services, making configuration simpler and less error-prone.

Popular Service Discovery Tools:

- Consul: A distributed key-value store that also provides service discovery, health checks, and configuration management.
- etcd: A distributed key-value store often used for service discovery in Kubernetes environments.
- ZooKeeper: A centralized service for maintaining configuration information, naming, providing distributed synchronization, and providing group services.

Load Balancing: Distributing Traffic Efficiently

Now that your services can discover each other, you need a way to distribute traffic among the available instances of a service. This is where load balancing comes in.

Load balancing ensures that no single instance of a service becomes overwhelmed with requests. It distributes incoming traffic across multiple instances, improving performance, availability, and resilience.

Load Balancing Approaches:

- Server-Side Load Balancing: A dedicated load balancer (like Nginx or HAProxy) sits in front of your services and distributes incoming requests among the available instances. This is a common approach for external traffic coming into your application.
- Client-Side Load Balancing: Clients (or a service mesh) are responsible for choosing which service instance to send requests to. This approach can be more efficient, as it eliminates a single point of failure (the load balancer) and allows for more intelligent routing decisions based on factors like service health and latency.

Load Balancing Algorithms:

Load balancers use various algorithms to distribute traffic, such as:

- Round Robin: Requests are distributed sequentially among the available instances.
- Least Connections: Requests are sent to the instance with the fewest active connections.
- IP Hash: Requests from the same client IP address are consistently sent to the same instance.

Real-World Examples

Service discovery and load balancing are essential components of many microservices architectures:

- Netflix: Uses Eureka for service discovery and Ribbon for client-side load balancing.
- Amazon: Relies heavily on service discovery and load balancing to manage its vast e-commerce platform.
- Kubernetes: Provides built-in service discovery and load balancing mechanisms for containerized applications.

Code Example (Conceptual):

While implementing service discovery and load balancing often involves using specific tools and libraries, here's a conceptual example of how a service might register itself with a service discovery system:

```go
Go

// ... (Connect to the service discovery system)
...

// Register the service

service := Service{

  Name: "my-service",

  Address: "192.168.1.10:8080",

}

err := serviceDiscovery.Register(service)

if err != nil {

  // Handle error

}
```

This code snippet illustrates the basic idea of registering a service with its name and address. In a real-world scenario, you would use a specific service discovery library like Consul or etcd to perform this registration.

By understanding service discovery and load balancing, you can build microservices architectures that are scalable, resilient, and able to handle the demands of modern applications. These concepts are crucial for managing the dynamic nature of microservices and ensuring that your application remains responsive and available.

Chapter 5: Concurrency in Go

Concurrency is the ability of a program to handle multiple tasks seemingly at the same time. It's like having a team of chefs in a kitchen, each working on a different part of a meal simultaneously, making the whole cooking process much faster.

Go has a unique and elegant approach to concurrency, built around two key concepts: goroutines and channels. These features make it surprisingly easy to write concurrent programs that are efficient, safe, and easy to understand.

5.1 Goroutines

Goroutines are the key to writing concurrent programs in Go, allowing you to perform multiple tasks seemingly at the same time, making your applications more efficient and responsive.

Think of a program as a chef in a kitchen. In a traditional program, the chef can only work on one dish at a time. If they need to chop vegetables, they have to finish chopping before they can start cooking the sauce. This sequential execution can be slow and inefficient, especially when dealing with multiple tasks.

Goroutines change this by allowing the chef to "delegate" tasks. A goroutine is like hiring an assistant chef who can work on a separate task concurrently. While the main chef is cooking the sauce, the assistant can chop vegetables, prepare the garnish, or do other tasks simultaneously. This parallel execution makes the whole cooking process much faster.

In Go, you can create a goroutine by simply adding the go keyword before a function call:

```
go myFunction() // This starts myFunction in a
new goroutine
```

This line of code tells Go to execute myFunction() concurrently in a separate goroutine. The main program continues to execute while myFunction() runs in the background. It's like the main chef continuing to cook the sauce while the assistant chef works on other tasks.

Why Goroutines are Lightweight

Goroutines are incredibly lightweight compared to traditional threads. A typical thread might consume several megabytes of memory, while a goroutine starts with just a few kilobytes. This means you can create thousands, even millions, of goroutines without overwhelming your system's resources.

Go achieves this efficiency through a technique called **multiplexing**. The Go runtime manages a pool of operating system threads and intelligently distributes goroutines among those threads. This allows many goroutines to share the same operating system thread, minimizing the overhead of context switching and memory usage.

Example: Concurrent Web Server

Let's see a practical example of how goroutines can improve the performance of a web server. In a traditional web server, each incoming request is handled sequentially. If one request takes a long time to process (e.g., fetching data from a slow database), it can block other requests, making the server less responsive.

With goroutines, you can handle each incoming request in a separate goroutine. This allows the server to process multiple requests concurrently, even if some requests take longer to complete.

```go
Go

package main

import (

    "fmt"

    "log"

    "net/http"

    "time"

)

func handler(w http.ResponseWriter, r *http.Request) {

    // Simulate a long-running task

    time.Sleep(2 * time.Second)

    fmt.Fprintln(w, "Hello from the server!")

}

func main() {

    http.HandleFunc("/", func(w http.ResponseWriter, r *http.Request) {

        go handler(w, r) // Handle each request in a separate goroutine

    })
```

```
log.Println("Server listening on port 8080")

log.Fatal(http.ListenAndServe(":8080", nil))
}
```

In this code:

- We define a handler function that simulates a long-running task (sleeping for 2 seconds) before sending a response.
- In the main function, we use http.HandleFunc to register a handler for the root path ("/").
- Inside the handler, we use go handler(w, r) to launch a new goroutine for each incoming request.

This way, even if one request takes a long time to process, other requests can be handled concurrently without being blocked.

Real-World Examples

Goroutines are used extensively in various Go applications and systems:

- Docker: The core of Docker, the popular containerization platform, is written in Go and heavily utilizes goroutines for managing containers and orchestrating their interactions.
- Kubernetes: Kubernetes, the leading container orchestration system, is also built with Go and relies on goroutines for handling complex tasks like scheduling, networking, and resource management.
- Go Web Servers: Many popular Go web frameworks, like Gin and Echo, use goroutines to handle concurrent requests and build high-performance web servers.

5.2 Channels

While goroutines allow you to execute tasks concurrently, channels provide a way for those goroutines to communicate and synchronize their actions. Think of channels as pipelines that connect goroutines, enabling them to send and receive data safely and efficiently.

Imagine a factory with multiple workers (goroutines) performing different tasks. Channels act as conveyor belts that transport materials (data) between those workers. One worker might place a finished product on the conveyor belt (send data to the channel), and another worker might pick it up from the belt (receive data from the channel) to perform the next step in the manufacturing process.

Creating Channels

You can create a channel in Go using the make() function and specifying the type of data that the channel will carry:

```Go
ch := make(chan int)  // Create a channel to send and receive integers
```

This line of code creates a channel named ch that can transport integer values. You can create channels for any data type, including structs, maps, and even other channels.

Sending and Receiving Data

To send a value to a channel, you use the <- operator:

```Go
ch <- 42 // Send the value 42 to the channel
```

This line sends the value 42 to the channel ch. If there's no goroutine waiting to receive the value, the sending goroutine will block until a receiver is available.

To receive a value from a channel:

```Go
value := <-ch // Receive a value from the channel
and store it in 'value'
```

This line receives a value from the channel ch and stores it in the variable value. If there's no value available in the channel, the receiving goroutine will block until a sender sends a value.

Example: Synchronizing Goroutines

Let's see a simple example of how to use channels to synchronize goroutines. We'll create two goroutines: one that prints "ping" and another that prints "pong." We'll use a channel to ensure that they print in the correct order ("ping" followed by "pong").

```Go
package main

import (

    "fmt"

    "time"

)

func pinger(ch chan string) {

    for i := 0; ; i++ {

        ch <- "ping" // Send "ping" to the
channel

        time.Sleep(time.Second)
```

```go
        }

    }

func ponger(ch chan string) {

    for i := 0; ; i++ {

        msg := <-ch // Receive a message from
the channel

        fmt.Println(msg)

        time.Sleep(time.Second)

    }

}

func main() {

    ch := make(chan string)

    go pinger(ch)

    go ponger(ch)

    fmt.Scanln() // Keep the main goroutine
alive

}
```

In this code:

- The pinger goroutine sends "ping" to the channel ch.
- The ponger goroutine receives a message from the channel ch and prints it.

- The channel ensures that "ping" is always printed before "pong" because the ponger goroutine has to wait for a value to be sent to the channel before it can proceed.

Buffered Channels

By default, channels are unbuffered, meaning that a send operation will block until a receiver is ready to receive the value. You can create buffered channels that can hold a certain number of values before blocking the sender.

Go

```go
ch := make(chan int, 3) // Create a buffered
channel with a capacity of 3
```

This creates a channel that can hold up to 3 integer values. Send operations to this channel will only block if the channel is already full.

Closing Channels

When you're done with a channel, you can close it using the close() function:

Go

```go
close(ch)
```

Closing a channel signals to receivers that no more values will be sent on the channel. You can use the for range loop to iterate over values received from a channel until it's closed.

Real-World Examples

Channels are used in various Go applications and systems:

- Worker Pools: Channels are used to distribute tasks among worker goroutines in a worker pool pattern.

- Message Queues: Channels can be used to implement message queues for asynchronous communication between services.
- Streaming Data: Channels can be used to stream data between goroutines, such as processing data from a sensor or reading data from a file.

By understanding and using channels effectively, you can control the flow of data between goroutines, synchronize their actions, and build concurrent programs that are efficient, safe, and easy to reason about.

5.3 Patterns for Concurrent Programming

When it comes to writing concurrent programs in Go, understanding some common patterns can greatly simplify your code and make it more robust and efficient. These patterns provide established solutions to recurring concurrency challenges, helping you structure your concurrent code in a way that's easy to understand, maintain, and scale.

Let's explore some of the most useful patterns for concurrent programming in Go.

1. Worker Pools

Think of a worker pool like a busy restaurant kitchen. You have a queue of orders (tasks) coming in, and a team of chefs (worker goroutines) ready to process those orders. The head chef (the main goroutine) distributes the orders among the chefs, ensuring that each chef has something to work on.

A worker pool pattern in Go involves creating a fixed number of worker goroutines that are ready to receive and process tasks from a channel. This helps limit the number of concurrent goroutines, preventing your program from overwhelming system resources.

Here's an example of a worker pool pattern:

Go

```go
package main

import (

    "fmt"

    "sync"

    "time"

)

func worker(id int, jobs <-chan int, results chan<- int) {

    for j := range jobs {

        fmt.Println("Worker", id, "started job", j)

        time.Sleep(time.Second) // Simulate some work

        fmt.Println("Worker", id, "finished job", j)

        results <- j * 2

    }

}

func main() {

    const numJobs = 5

    jobs := make(chan int, numJobs)
```

```go
    results := make(chan int, numJobs)

    // Create worker pool

    for w := 1; w <= 3; w++ {

        go worker(w, jobs, results)

    }

    // Send jobs

    for j := 1; j <= numJobs; j++ {

        jobs <- j

    }

    close(jobs)

    // Collect results

    for a := 1; a <= numJobs; a++ {

        <-results

    }

}
```

In this code:

- We create a worker function that receives jobs from the jobs channel, processes them, and sends the results to the results channel.
- We create a pool of 3 worker goroutines.
- We send 5 jobs to the jobs channel and then close it to signal that no more jobs are coming.
- We collect the results from the results channel.

2. Pipelines

A pipeline pattern is like an assembly line in a factory. Each worker on the line performs a specific task and passes the partially finished product to the next worker.

In Go, a pipeline involves a chain of goroutines where each goroutine performs a specific stage of processing and sends the data to the next stage via channels. This pattern is useful for breaking down complex tasks into smaller, more manageable steps.

Here's an example of a simple pipeline:

```Go
package main

import "fmt"

func stage1(in <-chan int, out chan<- int) {
	for num := range in {
		out <- num * 2 // Multiply the number by 2
	}
	close(out)
}

func stage2(in <-chan int, out chan<- int) {
	for num := range in {
		out <- num + 1 // Add 1 to the number
```

```go
    }

    close(out)

}

func main() {

    ch1 := make(chan int)

    ch2 := make(chan int)

    go stage1(ch1, ch2)

    go stage2(ch2, ch2)

    ch1 <- 1

    ch1 <- 2

    close(ch1)

    for result := range ch2 {

        fmt.Println(result) // Output: 3, 5

    }

}
```

In this code:

- stage1 multiplies the incoming number by 2 and sends it to ch2.
- stage2 receives the number from ch2, adds 1 to it, and sends it back to ch2.
- The main goroutine sends two numbers to ch1 and then closes it.

- The pipeline processes the numbers, and the results are printed from ch2.

3. Fan-out/Fan-in

The fan-out/fan-in pattern is useful for parallelizing tasks. In the fan-out stage, a single goroutine distributes tasks to multiple worker goroutines. In the fan-in stage, the results from those worker goroutines are collected and aggregated.

Here's a conceptual example:

```Go
// Fan-out: Distribute tasks to workers

for _, task := range tasks {

  go worker(task, results)

}

// Fan-in: Collect results from workers

for i := 0; i < len(tasks); i++ {

  result := <-results

  // Process the result

}
```

This pattern can be used for tasks like processing a large dataset in parallel or making multiple API calls concurrently.

Real-World Examples

These concurrency patterns are used in various real-world applications:

- Web Servers: Worker pools are often used in web servers to handle concurrent requests efficiently.
- Data Processing Pipelines: Pipelines are used to process data in stages, such as filtering, transforming, and aggregating data.
- Parallel Computations: Fan-out/fan-in is used to parallelize computations, such as image processing or scientific simulations.

5.4 Best Practices for Concurrency

Concurrency in Go, with its goroutines and channels, is a powerful tool for building efficient and responsive applications. However, it also introduces complexities that can lead to subtle bugs if not handled carefully. Let's discuss some best practices for writing concurrent Go code that is safe, reliable, and maintainable.

1. Avoid Data Races

One of the most common pitfalls in concurrent programming is data races. A data race occurs when multiple goroutines access and modify the same shared data concurrently without proper synchronization. This can lead to unpredictable and difficult-to-debug behavior, as the final state of the data depends on the unpredictable timing of goroutine execution.

To prevent data races, you need to synchronize access to shared data using mechanisms like:

- Channels: Channels provide a safe and synchronized way to communicate data between goroutines. By sending and receiving data through channels, you ensure that only one goroutine accesses the data at a time.
- Mutexes: A mutex (mutual exclusion) is like a lock that protects shared data. Only one goroutine can hold the lock

at a time, ensuring exclusive access to the data. Go's sync package provides sync.Mutex for this purpose.

```go
Go

package main

import (

    "fmt"

    "sync"

    "time"

)

type Counter struct {

    mu      sync.Mutex

    value int

}

func (c *Counter) Increment() {

    c.mu.Lock() // Acquire the lock

    defer c.mu.Unlock() // Release the lock when
the function exits

    c.value++

}

func main() {

    counter := Counter{}
```

```go
    for i := 0; i < 1000; i++ {

        go counter.Increment()

    }

    time.Sleep(time.Millisecond * 100) // Wait
for goroutines to finish

    fmt.Println("Counter:", counter.value) //
Should print 1000

}
```

In this code:

- We use a sync.Mutex to protect the value field of the Counter struct.
- The Increment() method acquires the lock before accessing and modifying the value, ensuring that only one goroutine can increment the counter at a time.

2. Keep Goroutines Short-Lived

Avoid creating long-running goroutines that might hold resources indefinitely. Ideally, goroutines should have a clear exit condition or a way to be signaled to stop. This prevents resource leaks and ensures that your program can terminate gracefully.

You can use channels to signal goroutines to stop:

```go
Go

func worker(stop <-chan bool) {

    for {

        select {
```

```
        case <-stop:

            fmt.Println("Stopping worker")

            return

        default:

            // Do some work

        }

    }

}

func main() {

    stop := make(chan bool)

    go worker(stop)

    // ... some time later ...

    stop <- true // Signal the worker to stop

}
```

In this code, the worker goroutine exits when it receives a value from the stop channel.

3. Limit Concurrency

While goroutines are lightweight, creating an excessive number of them can lead to resource exhaustion and performance degradation. Use techniques like worker pools or rate limiting to control the number of concurrent goroutines.

4. Handle Panics

A panic in a goroutine can crash the entire program if not handled properly. Use the recover() function within a deferred function to catch panics and prevent them from propagating.

```Go
func myFunction() {

    defer func() {

        if r := recover(); r != nil {

            fmt.Println("Recovered from
panic:", r)

        }

    }()

    // ... code that might panic ...

}
```

5. Test Concurrency Thoroughly

Concurrency can introduce subtle bugs that are difficult to reproduce. Write comprehensive tests, including unit tests and integration tests, to ensure that your concurrent code behaves correctly under different conditions. Use tools like Go's race detector to help identify potential data races.

Real-World Examples

These best practices are crucial in real-world concurrent applications:

- Web Servers: Handling concurrent requests safely and efficiently is essential for web server performance and stability.

- Data Pipelines: Synchronizing access to shared data in data pipelines prevents data corruption and ensures correct processing.
- Concurrent Algorithms: Implementing concurrent algorithms requires careful consideration of data races and synchronization to ensure correctness.

By following these best practices, you can write concurrent Go code that is not only efficient and responsive but also safe, reliable, and maintainable.

Chapter 6: Cloud Platforms and Deployment

Cloud platforms provide the infrastructure and tools to deploy, run, and scale your applications, making them accessible to users across the globe. They offer a range of services, from virtual machines and storage to databases and networking, allowing you to focus on building your application logic without worrying about the underlying infrastructure.

In this chapter, we'll explore the major cloud providers, learn how to containerize your Go applications with Docker, orchestrate them with Kubernetes, and deploy them to the cloud.

6.1 Introduction to Cloud Providers

Let's talk about the giants that power much of the internet today: cloud providers. These companies offer a vast array of computing resources and services over the internet, allowing you to deploy, run, and scale your applications without having to manage your own physical infrastructure. It's like renting a fully equipped kitchen instead of building one from scratch – you get all the tools and appliances you need, and you can focus on cooking (building your application) instead of worrying about plumbing and electricity.

Three major players dominate the cloud computing landscape: Amazon Web Services (AWS), Microsoft Azure, and Google Cloud Platform (GCP). Each provider offers a comprehensive suite of services, but they have their own strengths, weaknesses, and areas of focus.

Amazon Web Services (AWS)

AWS is the pioneer and current market leader in cloud computing. It was launched in 2006 and has since grown into a massive platform with hundreds of services covering virtually every aspect of cloud computing.

Some of its core services include:

- Compute: EC2 (Elastic Compute Cloud) provides virtual machines that you can use to run your applications.
- Storage: S3 (Simple Storage Service) offers scalable object storage for storing data like images, videos, and backups.
- Databases: RDS (Relational Database Service) provides managed relational databases (like MySQL, PostgreSQL, and SQL Server), and DynamoDB offers a NoSQL database service.
- Networking: VPC (Virtual Private Cloud) allows you to create isolated networks within AWS, and Route 53 provides DNS services.
- Serverless: Lambda allows you to run code without provisioning or managing servers.

AWS is known for its:

- Mature Ecosystem: A vast and mature ecosystem of services and tools.
- Wide Adoption: Used by many large companies and organizations.
- Global Reach: Data centers in numerous regions around the world.

However, AWS can also be:

- Complex: The sheer number of services and pricing options can be overwhelming.
- Costly: While AWS offers competitive pricing, it can become expensive if not managed carefully.

Microsoft Azure

Azure is Microsoft's cloud platform. Launched in 2010, it has rapidly grown to become a strong competitor to AWS. Azure is tightly integrated with the Microsoft ecosystem, making it a natural choice for organizations that rely on Windows Server, .NET, and other Microsoft technologies.

Some of its key services include:

- Compute: Virtual Machines offer a range of virtual machine sizes and operating systems.
- Storage: Blob Storage provides scalable object storage.
- Databases: SQL Database offers managed relational databases, and Cosmos DB provides a globally distributed, multi-model database service.
- Serverless: Azure Functions allows you to run code without managing servers.
- DevOps: Azure DevOps provides a suite of tools for development, testing, and deployment.

Azure is known for its:

- Strong Enterprise Focus: Good integration with Microsoft technologies and enterprise solutions.
- Hybrid Cloud Capabilities: Facilitates integration between on-premises infrastructure and Azure services.
- Competitive Pricing: Offers various pricing options and discounts.

However, Azure:

- May lack the breadth of services compared to AWS.
- Can have a steeper learning curve for those unfamiliar with the Microsoft ecosystem.

Google Cloud Platform (GCP)

GCP is Google's cloud offering. Launched in 2011, it has gained significant traction, particularly in areas like data analytics, machine learning, and Kubernetes.

Some of its core services include:

- Compute: Compute Engine provides virtual machines.
- Storage: Cloud Storage offers scalable object storage.
- Databases: Cloud SQL provides managed relational databases, and Cloud Spanner offers a globally distributed, scalable database service.
- Big Data: BigQuery is a serverless, highly scalable data warehouse for analytics.
- Machine Learning: Offers various machine learning services, including pre-trained models and custom model training.
- Kubernetes: GKE (Google Kubernetes Engine) is a managed Kubernetes service.

GCP is known for its:

- Data Analytics and Machine Learning: Strong capabilities in these areas, leveraging Google's expertise.
- Kubernetes: GKE is considered one of the best Kubernetes offerings.
- Competitive Pricing: Often offers aggressive pricing and sustained use discounts.

However, GCP:

- May have a smaller market share and ecosystem compared to AWS and Azure.
- Can have a learning curve for those unfamiliar with Google's technologies.

Real-World Examples

- Netflix: Uses AWS extensively for its streaming platform.
- Spotify: Uses GCP for its data infrastructure and machine learning.
- eBay: Uses a combination of AWS and Azure for its e-commerce platform.

Choosing the right cloud provider depends on your specific needs and priorities. Consider factors like the services offered, pricing, regions, support, and ecosystem. It's also common for companies to use a multi-cloud strategy, leveraging services from multiple providers to optimize costs and leverage specific strengths.

6.2 Containerization with Docker

Docker provides a way to containerize your applications, bundling them with all their dependencies into a standardized unit called a container. This container can then be run on any system that has Docker installed, regardless of the underlying operating system or infrastructure.

Think of it like shipping goods overseas. You wouldn't just throw all your items loosely into a ship's cargo hold, would you? You would pack them carefully into standardized containers, ensuring they are protected and organized during transportation. Docker does the same for your applications, packaging them into containers that can be easily moved and run anywhere.

Why Use Docker?

- Consistency: Your application runs the same way in every environment – development, testing, staging, and production. This eliminates the "it works on my machine" problem, where applications behave differently in different environments due to variations in dependencies or configurations.
- Portability: Docker containers can run on any system with Docker installed, whether it's your laptop, a server in your

data center, or a cloud instance. This makes it easy to move your applications between environments.

- Isolation: Containers provide isolation, meaning that applications running in different containers don't interfere with each other. This improves security and stability.
- Efficiency: Docker images are built in layers, making them efficient to store and transfer. Only the changed layers need to be transferred when updating an image, saving time and bandwidth.

Docker Concepts

- Docker Image: A read-only template that contains your application code, dependencies, and configurations. It's like a blueprint for your container.
- Docker Container: A running instance of a Docker image. It's like a self-contained virtual environment where your application executes.
- Dockerfile: A text file that contains instructions for building a Docker image. It specifies the base image, dependencies, application code, and other configurations.
- Docker Hub: A public registry for storing and sharing Docker images. You can find pre-built images for various applications and frameworks, or you can push your own images to share with others.

Building a Docker Image for Your Go Application

To containerize your Go application, you need to create a Dockerfile. This file contains instructions for building a Docker image that includes your application code and all its dependencies.

Here's an example of a Dockerfile for a simple Go web application:

```
Dockerfile
```

```
FROM golang:1.19-alpine AS builder

WORKDIR /app

COPY go.mod ./

COPY go.sum ./

RUN go mod download

COPY . .

RUN go build -o main .

# ---

FROM alpine:latest

RUN apk --no-cache add ca-certificates

WORKDIR /app

COPY --from=builder /app/main .

CMD ["./main"]
```

Let's break down this Dockerfile:

- **FROM golang:1.19-alpine AS builder**: This line specifies the base image for the build stage. We're using the official Go image (golang:1.19-alpine), which includes the Go toolchain and is based on the lightweight Alpine Linux distribution. We name this stage "builder".
- **WORKDIR /app**: This sets the working directory within the image to /app.
- **COPY go.mod ./** and **COPY go.sum ./**: These lines copy the go.mod and go.sum files from your project directory into the image's working directory. These files define your project's dependencies.

- RUN go mod download: This line downloads the project's dependencies.
- COPY . .: This copies the rest of your application code into the image.
- RUN go build -o main .: This line builds your Go application, producing an executable named main.
- FROM alpine:latest: This starts a new stage for the final image, using a minimal base image (alpine:latest) to reduce the image size.
- RUN apk --no-cache add ca-certificates: This installs the ca-certificates package, which is needed for making HTTPS requests.
- WORKDIR /app: Sets the working directory for the final image.
- COPY --from=builder /app/main .: This copies the built executable (main) from the "builder" stage into the final image.
- CMD ["./main"]: This sets the default command to run when the container starts. In this case, it runs the main executable.

Building and Running the Docker Image

To build the Docker image, you use the docker build command:

```bash
Bash

docker build -t my-go-app .
```

This command builds an image tagged as my-go-app. The -t flag specifies the tag for the image. The . at the end specifies the build context, which is the current directory.

To run the Docker image:

```bash
Bash
```

```
docker run -p 8080:8080 my-go-app
```

This command runs the container and maps port 8080 of the container to port 8080 of the host machine. This allows you to access your Go application running inside the container by visiting localhost:8080 in your web browser.

Real-World Examples

Docker is used extensively in various industries and applications:

- Web Development: Deploying web applications in containers ensures consistency and portability across different environments.
- Microservices: Packaging microservices in containers allows for independent deployment and scaling.
- DevOps: Docker is a key component of many DevOps pipelines, enabling automated builds, testing, and deployments.
- Cloud Platforms: Cloud providers like AWS, Azure, and GCP offer container services that integrate seamlessly with Docker.

6.3 Orchestration with Kubernetes

Kubernetes is a powerful platform for orchestrating and managing containerized applications. While Docker helps you package your applications into containers, Kubernetes takes it a step further by automating the deployment, scaling, and management of those containers.

Think of it like this: you have a fleet of delivery trucks (containers) carrying goods (your application). Kubernetes acts as the logistics center, managing the routes, scheduling deliveries, ensuring the trucks are in good condition, and scaling the fleet up or down based on demand.

Kubernetes originated at Google, where it was born out of the company's experience managing containers at a massive scale. It has since become the de facto standard for container orchestration, offering a robust and flexible platform for running containerized applications.

Why Use Kubernetes?

- Automated Deployment: Kubernetes automates the deployment of your containers, ensuring they are scheduled on the right machines and configured correctly.
- Scalability: Kubernetes makes it easy to scale your application up or down by adding or removing container instances based on demand. This ensures that your application can handle varying workloads and traffic.
- Self-Healing: Kubernetes monitors the health of your containers and automatically restarts or replaces any containers that fail. This improves the resilience and availability of your application.
- Service Discovery: Kubernetes provides built-in service discovery, allowing your services to find and communicate with each other easily.
- Rolling Updates: Kubernetes can perform rolling updates, gradually deploying new versions of your application without downtime.

Kubernetes Concepts

To understand how Kubernetes works, let's explore some key concepts:

- **Cluster:** A set of machines (nodes) that run your containerized applications. It's like a data center where your containers reside.

- Node: A physical or virtual machine within a Kubernetes cluster. Each node has the necessary resources (CPU, memory, storage) to run containers.
- Pod: The smallest deployable unit in Kubernetes. A pod can contain one or more containers that share the same network and storage resources. It's like a group of containers that work together.
- Deployment: A Kubernetes object that manages the rollout and updates of your application. It ensures that the desired number of pods are running and that they are updated to the latest version of your application.
- Service: An abstraction that defines a logical set of pods and a policy for accessing them. It provides a stable endpoint for accessing your application, even if the underlying pods change.
- Namespace: A way to divide a Kubernetes cluster into logical partitions. You can use namespaces to isolate different environments (development, staging, production) or teams within the same cluster.

Deploying to Kubernetes

Deploying your Go application to Kubernetes involves creating YAML configuration files that define your deployments, services, and other Kubernetes resources. These files describe how your application should be deployed, scaled, and accessed.

Here's an example of a deployment configuration file:

```YAML
apiVersion: apps/v1

kind: Deployment

metadata:
```

```yaml
  name: my-go-app

spec:

  replicas: 3 # Number of desired pods

  selector:

    matchLabels:

      app: my-go-app # Label to select pods

  template:

    metadata:

      labels:

        app: my-go-app

    spec:

      containers:

      - name: my-go-app

        image: my-go-app:latest # Docker image to
use

        ports:

        - containerPort: 8080 # Port the
application listens on
```

This configuration defines a deployment named my-go-app that runs 3 replicas of your Go application container. The selector field specifies that this deployment manages pods with the label app: my-go-app. The template field defines the pod template, which includes the container specification (name, image, ports).

To deploy this configuration to Kubernetes, you use the kubectl apply command:

```bash
Bash

kubectl apply -f deployment.yaml
```

This command creates the deployment and starts the specified number of pods.

Real-World Examples

Kubernetes is used by many companies to manage their containerized applications:

- Spotify: Uses Kubernetes to manage its music streaming platform, handling millions of users and songs.
- Airbnb: Uses Kubernetes to deploy and scale its services, including search, payments, and user management.
- Pokémon Go: Uses Kubernetes to handle the massive scale and dynamic demands of its augmented reality game.

By learning Kubernetes, you gain a powerful tool for managing your Go applications in a cloud-native environment. It enables you to automate deployments, scale your applications efficiently, and ensure high availability and resilience.

6.4 Deploying Go Applications to the Cloud

Deploying your application to the cloud allows you to make it accessible to users everywhere, ensuring scalability, reliability, and efficient resource utilization.

Let's break down the process of deploying your Go application to the cloud, combining the knowledge we've gained about cloud providers, Docker, and Kubernetes.

1. Choose a Cloud Provider

The first step is to select a cloud provider that meets your needs. The major cloud providers – AWS, Azure, and GCP – offer a variety of services and pricing models. Consider factors like the services you need, your budget, the regions where your users are located, and your existing technology stack when making your choice.

2. Containerize Your Application

Next, you need to package your Go application into a Docker container. This involves creating a Dockerfile that specifies the base image, dependencies, application code, and other configurations.

Here's a recap of the basic steps:

- Create a Dockerfile in your project directory.
- Specify a base image (e.g., golang:1.19-alpine).
- Copy your application code and dependencies into the image.
- Build the Docker image using the docker build command.

3. Push the Image to a Registry

Once you have a Docker image, you need to store it in a container registry. This allows your cloud provider to access and pull the image when deploying your application.

Popular container registries include:

- Docker Hub: A public registry where you can store and share Docker images.
- Amazon ECR (Elastic Container Registry): AWS's container registry.
- Azure Container Registry: Azure's container registry.
- Google Container Registry: GCP's container registry.

To push your image to a registry, you first need to tag it with the registry's URL and your credentials. For example, to push to Docker Hub:

```Bash
docker tag my-go-app:latest
your-dockerhub-username/my-go-app:latest

docker push
your-dockerhub-username/my-go-app:latest
```

4. Create a Kubernetes Cluster

Kubernetes is the recommended platform for orchestrating and managing your containerized applications in the cloud. Each cloud provider offers managed Kubernetes services:

- AWS: EKS (Elastic Kubernetes Service)
- Azure: AKS (Azure Kubernetes Service)
- GCP: GKE (Google Kubernetes Engine)

These services make it easy to create and manage Kubernetes clusters without having to worry about the underlying infrastructure.

5. Deploy Your Application

Once you have a Kubernetes cluster, you can deploy your Go application using Kubernetes configuration files. These files define your deployments, services, and other Kubernetes resources.

Here's a basic example of a deployment configuration:

```YAML
apiVersion: apps/v1

kind: Deployment
```

```yaml
metadata:
  name: my-go-app
spec:
  replicas: 3
  selector:
    matchLabels:
      app: my-go-app
  template:
    metadata:
      labels:
        app: my-go-app
    spec:
      containers:
      - name: my-go-app
        image: your-dockerhub-username/my-go-app:latest # Use the image from the registry
        ports:
        - containerPort: 8080
```

This configuration defines a deployment that runs 3 replicas of your Go application container, using the image you pushed to the registry.

You can deploy this configuration using the kubectl apply command:

```Bash

kubectl apply -f deployment.yaml
```

6. Expose Your Application

To make your application accessible to users, you need to expose it through a Kubernetes service. A service provides a stable endpoint for accessing your application, even if the underlying pods change.

Here's an example of a service configuration:

```YAML

apiVersion: v1

kind: Service

metadata:

  name: my-go-app-service

spec:

  selector:

    app: my-go-app

  ports:

  - protocol: TCP

    port: 80

    targetPort: 8080

  type: LoadBalancer
```

This configuration defines a service that exposes your application on port 80, forwarding traffic to port 8080 of the pods with the label app: my-go-app. The type: LoadBalancer tells Kubernetes to create a load balancer that distributes traffic to the pods.

7. Access Your Application

Once the service is created, Kubernetes will assign it an external IP address. You can then access your application using this IP address or a domain name that you configure to point to it.

Real-World Examples

Many companies use this approach to deploy their Go applications to the cloud:

- Shopify: Uses Kubernetes to manage its e-commerce platform, handling millions of merchants and transactions.
- Pinterest: Uses Kubernetes to deploy and scale its image-sharing platform, serving billions of pins and recommendations.
- Twitch: Uses Kubernetes to power its live streaming platform, handling millions of concurrent viewers and broadcasters.

By following these steps, you can successfully deploy your Go applications to the cloud, leveraging the power of containerization, orchestration, and cloud infrastructure to create scalable, reliable, and highly available applications.

Chapter 7: Building Scalable and Resilient Systems

In this chapter, we'll explore techniques for building scalable and resilient systems. We'll discuss how to handle increasing traffic with load balancing and caching, how to use message queues for asynchronous communication, and how to implement robust error handling, logging, monitoring, and observability. Think of this as equipping your application with the armor and tools it needs to thrive in the wild.

7.1 Scaling Techniques

As your Go application starts handling real-world traffic, you'll need to ensure it can gracefully handle increasing demand. This is where scaling comes in. Scaling means adding more resources to your application to accommodate growth in users, traffic, or data. It's like expanding your restaurant to accommodate more diners – you might add more tables, hire more staff, and even open new locations to handle the increased demand.

Two essential techniques for scaling web applications are load balancing and caching. Let's explore each of them in detail.

Load Balancing

Imagine a single waiter trying to serve a packed restaurant. They would be overwhelmed, running back and forth, leading to slow service and frustrated customers. The solution? Hire more waiters to distribute the workload!

Load balancing does the same for your application. It distributes incoming network traffic across multiple servers (or instances of your application), preventing any single server from becoming overloaded. This ensures that your application remains responsive and performs well even under heavy traffic.

Here are some common load balancing approaches:

- Server-Side Load Balancing: This involves using a dedicated load balancer appliance or software (like Nginx, HAProxy, or cloud provider load balancers) that sits in front of your servers. The load balancer receives incoming requests and distributes them across the available servers based on factors like server load, health checks, and configured rules. This is a common approach for handling external traffic coming into your application.
- Client-Side Load Balancing: In this approach, the client (or a service mesh) is responsible for choosing which server to send the request to. This can be more efficient, as it eliminates a single point of failure (the load balancer) and allows for more intelligent routing decisions based on factors like server proximity, latency, and health.
- DNS Load Balancing: DNS (Domain Name System) can be used to distribute traffic across multiple servers. When a client requests the IP address of your application's domain name, the DNS server can return different IP addresses for different requests, effectively distributing the traffic among those servers.

Load Balancing Algorithms

Load balancers use various algorithms to decide how to distribute traffic. Some common algorithms include:

- Round Robin: Requests are distributed sequentially to each server in a rotating manner.
- Least Connections: Requests are sent to the server with the fewest active connections.
- IP Hash: Requests from the same client IP address are consistently sent to the same server. This can be useful for maintaining session persistence.

- Weighted Round Robin: Similar to round robin, but each server is assigned a weight, and requests are distributed proportionally to those weights. This allows you to give more powerful servers a larger share of the traffic.

Benefits of Load Balancing

- Improved Performance: Distributing the workload prevents any single server from being overwhelmed, resulting in faster response times and improved performance.
- Increased Scalability: Load balancing allows you to easily scale your application horizontally by adding more servers to handle increased traffic.
- High Availability: If one server fails, the load balancer can automatically redirect traffic to other healthy servers, ensuring that your application remains available.
- Fault Tolerance: Load balancing provides fault tolerance by distributing the risk across multiple servers.

Caching

Caching is like keeping frequently used ingredients readily available in a kitchen. Instead of going to the grocery store (database or backend systems) every time you need an onion (data), you keep a few on the counter for quick access.

In web applications, caching involves storing frequently accessed data in a cache, which is a temporary storage area that is faster to access than the original data source. When a request comes in for that data, the cache is checked first. If the data is found in the cache (a cache hit), it's returned immediately, saving a trip to the database or other backend systems.

Types of Caching

- Browser Caching: Static assets like images, CSS files, and JavaScript files can be cached in the user's browser, so they don't have to be downloaded every time the user visits your website.

- CDN (Content Delivery Network) Caching: CDNs store copies of your content on servers located around the world. When a user requests your content, the CDN serves it from the server closest to the user, reducing latency and improving performance.
- Server-Side Caching: Your application server can cache frequently accessed data in memory (using tools like Redis or Memcached) or on disk.
- Database Caching: Databases often have built-in caching mechanisms to store frequently accessed data in memory.

Benefits of Caching

- Reduced Latency: Caching reduces the time it takes to retrieve data, resulting in faster response times and improved user experience.
- Reduced Server Load: Caching reduces the number of requests that need to be processed by your servers, freeing up resources to handle other tasks.
- Improved Scalability: Caching can help your application handle more traffic by reducing the load on your backend systems.
- Reduced Costs: Caching can reduce your infrastructure costs by reducing the need for more powerful servers or databases.

Real-World Examples

Load balancing and caching are used extensively by companies like:

- Facebook: Uses load balancing to distribute traffic across its massive network of servers and caching to store frequently accessed data like user profiles and posts.

- Amazon: Uses load balancing and caching to handle millions of transactions and product searches on its e-commerce platform.
- Google: Uses load balancing and caching to serve search results, maps, and other content to billions of users worldwide.

7.2 Message Queues

Message queues are powerful tools for building scalable and resilient applications. Message queues provide a way for different parts of your application, or even different applications altogether, to communicate asynchronously. It's like leaving a message for someone instead of calling them directly. The message waits in the queue until the recipient is ready to retrieve and process it.

This asynchronous communication style offers several benefits, especially when dealing with complex systems or high-volume data.

Why Use Message Queues?

- Decoupling: Message queues decouple different parts of your system, allowing them to operate independently without direct dependencies. This means that if one part of the system is slow or unavailable, it won't directly affect other parts.
- Scalability: Message queues can handle large volumes of messages and distribute them efficiently among consumers. This makes them ideal for scaling applications that need to process a high volume of data or requests.
- Resilience: Message queues can store messages durably, ensuring that they are not lost even if a consumer or other part of the system fails. This improves the reliability and fault tolerance of your application.

- Flexibility: Message queues support various messaging patterns, such as point-to-point, publish-subscribe, and request-response, allowing you to choose the best approach for your needs.

Popular Message Queue Systems

Two popular message queue systems are RabbitMQ and Kafka.

RabbitMQ

RabbitMQ is a versatile and mature message broker that supports various messaging protocols and features. It's known for its flexibility and ease of use, making it a good choice for a wide range of applications.

Key features of RabbitMQ include:

- Multiple Messaging Protocols: Supports AMQP (Advanced Message Queuing Protocol), MQTT (Message Queuing Telemetry Transport), and STOMP (Simple Text Oriented Messaging Protocol).
- Flexible Routing: Offers various routing options, allowing you to deliver messages to specific queues or consumers based on rules and patterns.
- Message Acknowledgements: Ensures that messages are processed successfully by requiring consumers to acknowledge them.
- High Availability: Provides features for clustering and high availability to ensure message delivery even if a node fails.

Kafka

Kafka is a high-throughput, distributed streaming platform designed to handle large volumes of data. It's often used for real-time data pipelines, event streaming, and log aggregation.

Key features of Kafka include:

- High Throughput: Can handle massive volumes of data with high throughput and low latency.
- Fault Tolerance: Distributes data across multiple brokers for fault tolerance and high availability.
- Scalability: Can easily scale horizontally by adding more brokers to the cluster.
- Persistent Storage: Stores messages durably on disk, ensuring that they are not lost.

The choice between RabbitMQ and Kafka depends on your specific needs:

- Versatility and Ease of Use: If you need a versatile message broker with a wide range of features and easy setup, RabbitMQ is a good choice.
- High Throughput and Scalability: If you need to handle massive volumes of data with high throughput and scalability, Kafka is a better fit.

Code Example: Using RabbitMQ with Go

Here's a basic example of how to publish and consume messages using RabbitMQ with Go:

```Go
package main

import (

    "fmt"

    "log"

    "github.com/streadway/amqp"

)
```

```go
func failOnError(err error, msg string) {

    if err != nil {

        log.Fatalf("%s: %s", msg, err)

    }

}

func main() {

    conn, err :=
amqp.Dial("amqp://guest:guest@localhost:5672/")

    failOnError(err, "Failed to connect to
RabbitMQ")

    defer conn.Close()

    ch, err := conn.Channel()

    failOnError(err, "Failed to open a channel")

    defer ch.Close()

    q, err := ch.QueueDeclare(

        "hello", // name

        false,   // durable

        false,   // delete when unused

        false,   // exclusive

        false,   // no-wait

        nil,     // arguments
```

```go
	)

	failOnError(err, "Failed to declare a
queue")

	body := "Hello World!"

	err = ch.Publish(
		"",       // exchange
		q.Name,   // routing key
		false,    // mandatory
		false,    // immediate
		amqp.Publishing{
			ContentType: "text/plain",
			Body:        []byte(body),
		})

	failOnError(err, "Failed to publish a
message")

	log.Printf(" [x] Sent %s\n", body)
}
```

This code connects to a RabbitMQ server, declares a queue named
"hello", and publishes a message to that queue. You would need a
separate consumer program to receive messages from the queue.

Real-World Examples

Message queues are used in various applications:

- E-commerce: Process orders asynchronously, send notifications, and update inventory.
- Social Media: Handle user activity streams, notifications, and message delivery.
- Financial Systems: Process transactions, update account balances, and generate reports.

7.3 Error Handling and Logging

In software development, errors are inevitable. No matter how carefully you write your code, there will always be unexpected situations, invalid inputs, or external factors that can cause your application to stumble. This is why robust error handling and logging are crucial for building reliable and maintainable Go applications.

Think of error handling and logging as your application's safety net and diagnostic tools. Error handling helps you gracefully recover from errors, preventing crashes and providing informative feedback to users. Logging provides a record of events, errors, and other important information, helping you understand what's happening within your application and diagnose issues when they arise.

Error Handling

The goal of error handling is to prevent errors from crashing your application and to provide users with helpful information about what went wrong. Here are some key principles to keep in mind:

- Handle Errors, Don't Ignore Them: When a function returns an error, don't just ignore it. Check for errors and handle them appropriately. This might involve retrying the operation, returning an error message to the user, or logging the error for later analysis.
- Provide Contextual Error Messages: Instead of generic error messages like "Something went wrong," provide specific

and informative messages that help users understand the nature of the error and how to potentially resolve it. For example, instead of "Invalid input," you might say "Invalid email address format."

- Distinguish Between Different Error Types: Categorize errors into different types (e.g., validation errors, database errors, network errors). This allows you to handle different types of errors differently and provide more specific error messages.
- Use Custom Error Types: Go allows you to define custom error types that can provide more context and information about the error. This can be useful for complex applications where you need to handle different types of errors in specific ways.

Example: Handling a Database Error

```Go
package main

import (

    "database/sql"

    "fmt"

    "log"

)

func getUser(db *sql.DB, userID int) (User,
error) {

    var user User
```

```go
    err := db.QueryRow("SELECT id, name, email
FROM users WHERE id = ?", userID).Scan(&user.ID,
&user.Name, &user.Email)

    if err != nil {

        if err == sql.ErrNoRows {

            return User{}, fmt.Errorf("user
with ID %d not found", userID) // Custom error
message

        }

        return User{}, fmt.Errorf("error
querying database: %w", err) // Wrap the original
error

    }

    return user, nil

}
```

In this code:

- We check for errors returned by db.QueryRow().
- If the error is sql.ErrNoRows, we return a custom error message indicating that the user was not found.
- Otherwise, we wrap the original error with a more informative message.

Logging

Logging provides a record of events, errors, and other important information that can help you understand what's happening within your application. Here are some logging best practices:

- Log Important Events: Log events like user logins, order placements, and other significant actions. This can help you track user activity and identify patterns.
- Log Errors with Context: When logging errors, include relevant context like timestamps, request IDs, user IDs, and any other information that can help you diagnose the issue.
- Use Structured Logging: Use a structured logging format (like JSON) instead of plain text. This makes it easier to search, filter, and analyze logs using tools like Elasticsearch or Splunk.
- Choose the Right Log Level: Use different log levels (e.g., debug, info, warning, error, critical) to categorize log messages based on their severity and importance.
- Centralize Logs: Use a centralized logging system to aggregate logs from different parts of your application or different servers. This provides a single place to view and analyze logs.

Example: Logging with Context

```go
Go

package main

import (

    "log"

    "net/http"

)

func handler(w http.ResponseWriter, r
*http.Request) {

    requestID := generateRequestID() // Generate
a unique ID for the request
```

```go
    log.Printf("[%s] Received request for %s",
requestID, r.URL.Path)

    // ... process the request ...

    if err != nil {

        log.Printf("[%s] Error processing
request: %v", requestID, err)

        http.Error(w, "Internal server error",
http.StatusInternalServerError)

        return

    }

    log.Printf("[%s] Successfully processed
request", requestID)

}
```

In this code:

- We generate a unique request ID.
- We log the request details and any errors that occur, including the request ID for context.

Real-World Examples

Error handling and logging are critical in production systems:

- E-commerce: Logging user actions, transactions, and errors helps track orders, identify fraudulent activity, and diagnose payment issues.
- Financial Systems: Robust error handling and logging are essential for ensuring the accuracy and integrity of financial transactions.

- Monitoring Systems: Logging system events and metrics helps identify performance bottlenecks, resource usage, and potential issues.

By implementing effective error handling and logging, you can build Go applications that are more reliable, maintainable, and easier to debug. These practices are essential for ensuring the stability and health of your applications in production environments.

7.4 Monitoring and Observability

Think of it like a doctor monitoring a patient's vital signs. By tracking metrics like heart rate, blood pressure, and temperature, the doctor can assess the patient's health and diagnose potential issues.[2] Similarly, monitoring and observability provide you with the tools to track the "vital signs" of your application, allowing you to identify bottlenecks, detect anomalies, and ensure everything is running smoothly.[3]

Monitoring

Monitoring involves collecting and tracking key metrics about your application's performance and health.[4] These metrics can include:

- Request Latency: The time it takes to process a request.
- Error Rates: The number of errors occurring in your application.[5]
- Request Throughput: The number of requests processed per second.
- Resource Utilization: The amount of CPU, memory, and disk space being used.[6]
- Uptime and Downtime: The availability of your application.

By tracking these metrics, you can:

- Identify Performance Bottlenecks: Spot areas where your application is slow or inefficient.[7]

- Detect Anomalies: Notice unusual patterns or spikes in metrics that might indicate problems.[8]
- Alert on Critical Issues: Set up alerts to notify you when critical metrics exceed thresholds.[9]
- Track Trends: Observe trends in metrics over time to understand how your application's performance is changing.

Tools for Monitoring

Several tools can help you collect and visualize metrics:

- Prometheus: A popular open-source monitoring system and time series database.[10]
- Grafana: A platform for visualizing metrics and creating dashboards.[11]
- Datadog: A commercial monitoring service that provides a wide range of integrations and features.[12]
- Cloud Provider Monitoring Services: AWS, Azure, and GCP offer their own monitoring services.[13]

Observability

Observability goes beyond basic monitoring by providing a deeper understanding of *why* things are happening in your application. It allows you to trace requests as they flow through your system, analyze logs to identify the root cause of errors, and profile your code to find performance bottlenecks.

Three pillars of observability are:

- Metrics: Quantitative data points that measure various aspects of your application's performance.[14]
- Traces: Records of requests as they flow through your system, showing the sequence of operations and the time spent in each component.[15]
- Logs: Detailed records of events and errors that occur in your application.[16]

Tools for Observability

- Jaeger: An open-source distributed tracing system.[17]
- Zipkin: Another popular open-source distributed tracing system.[18]
- ELK Stack (Elasticsearch, Logstash, Kibana): A powerful combination of tools for collecting, storing, and visualizing logs.[19]

Implementing Monitoring and Observability in Go

Go provides several libraries and tools for implementing monitoring and observability:[20]

- expvar package: Provides a standardized way to expose metrics from your Go application.[21]
- Prometheus client libraries: Allow you to instrument your Go code to collect and export Prometheus metrics.[22]
- OpenTelemetry: A collection of tools, APIs, and SDKs for generating and collecting telemetry data (metrics, traces, logs).[23]

Example: Exposing Metrics with expvar

```Go
package main

import (

    "expvar"

    "net/http"

)

var requestsCounter =
expvar.NewInt("requests_total")
```

```go
func handler(w http.ResponseWriter, r
*http.Request) {

    requestsCounter.Add(1) // Increment the
counter for each request

    // ... process the request ...

}

func main() {

    http.HandleFunc("/", handler)

    http.ListenAndServe(":8080", nil)

}
```

This code uses expvar to expose a counter that tracks the total number of requests. You can access this metric by visiting /debug/vars in your web browser.

Real-World Examples

Monitoring and observability are crucial for running applications at scale:

- Netflix: Uses a combination of monitoring and observability tools to track the performance of its streaming platform and ensure a seamless user experience.[24]
- Uber: Relies on observability to understand the complex interactions between its various microservices and diagnose issues quickly.[25]
- Etsy: Uses monitoring and observability to optimize the performance of its e-commerce platform and identify areas for improvement.[26]

By implementing monitoring and observability in your Go applications, you gain valuable insights into their behavior, performance, and health. This allows you to proactively identify and resolve issues, optimize performance, and ensure that your applications are running smoothly.[27]

Chapter 8: gRPC and Protocol Buffers

There's another powerful tool in the toolbox for inter-service communication, especially when performance and efficiency are paramount: gRPC. gRPC, combined with Protocol Buffers, offers a high-performance, type-safe, and language-agnostic framework for building distributed systems. Think of gRPC as a super-efficient courier service for your microservices. While REST is like sending messages through regular mail, gRPC is like using express delivery with optimized routes and streamlined packaging. In this chapter, we'll explore gRPC and Protocol Buffers, learn how to define services, build gRPC clients and servers, and see how gRPC fits into a microservices architecture.

8.1 Introduction to gRPC

While RESTful APIs with JSON are a common way to connect services, gRPC offers some significant advantages, especially when performance and efficiency are critical. Think of it like this: you need to send a package across the country. You could use regular mail (REST), which is widely used and generally reliable. But if you need to send something quickly and efficiently, you might choose a specialized courier service (gRPC) that offers optimized routes, faster delivery, and streamlined packaging.

gRPC (Google Remote Procedure Call) is an open-source framework developed by Google that allows you to build distributed systems where different services can communicate with each other as if they were local objects. It's like having a direct, high-speed connection between your services, enabling them to exchange data and trigger actions with minimal overhead.

How gRPC Works

gRPC combines several technologies to achieve its performance and efficiency:

- Protocol Buffers: Instead of using JSON for data exchange, gRPC uses Protocol Buffers (protobuf), a language-agnostic mechanism for serializing structured data. Protobuf is more compact and efficient than JSON, resulting in smaller message sizes and faster serialization/deserialization. This means less data needs to be transmitted over the network, leading to faster communication.
- HTTP/2: gRPC leverages HTTP/2, a modern transport protocol that offers several advantages over traditional HTTP/1.1. HTTP/2 features like multiplexing (sending multiple requests and responses over a single connection), header compression, and bidirectional streaming contribute to gRPC's performance and efficiency.
- Contract-First Approach: gRPC uses a contract-first approach, where you define the service interface and data structures in a Protocol Buffer definition file (.proto file). This file acts as a contract between the client and the server, clearly specifying the methods that can be called and the data that will be exchanged. This approach promotes clear interfaces and reduces errors due to mismatched expectations.

Benefits of gRPC

- Performance: gRPC's use of protobuf and HTTP/2 results in significantly faster communication compared to REST, especially for internal service-to-service communication where efficiency is crucial.
- Type Safety: The contract-first approach with protobuf ensures type safety, meaning that the client and server have a shared understanding of the data types being exchanged. This reduces errors caused by data type mismatches, which

can be common in systems that use loosely typed formats like JSON.

- Streaming: gRPC supports various types of streaming:
  - Server-side streaming: The server sends a stream of messages to the client.
  - Client-side streaming: The client sends a stream of messages to the server.
  - Bidirectional streaming: Both the client and server can send and receive streams of messages. This streaming capability is useful for scenarios like real-time updates, chat applications, or large data transfers.
- Language-Agnostic: gRPC supports a wide range of programming languages, including Go, Java, Python, C++, and Node.js. This makes it suitable for building polyglot systems where different services might be written in different languages.

Real-World Examples

gRPC is used in various applications and systems:

- Microservices Communication: Many companies use gRPC for internal communication between microservices, especially when performance and efficiency are critical.
- Cloud-Native Applications: gRPC is well-suited for cloud-native applications, as its efficiency and streaming capabilities align well with the demands of cloud environments.
- Real-time Applications: gRPC's streaming features make it a good choice for real-time applications like chat, video conferencing, and online gaming.
- API Gateways: Some API gateways use gRPC to communicate with backend services, improving performance and reducing latency.

8.2 Defining Services with Protocol Buffers

Let's discuss how to define gRPC services using Protocol Buffers, the language-agnostic mechanism for serializing structured data. Protocol Buffers, often referred to as "protobuf," provide a way to define the structure of the messages that your gRPC services will use to communicate.[1] It's like creating a blueprint for the data that will be exchanged between your client and server.

Think of it like this: you're designing a new type of electronic device. You wouldn't just start soldering components together randomly, would you? You would first create a detailed schematic that specifies the components, their connections, and how they interact. Protocol Buffers serve a similar purpose in gRPC, providing a clear and precise definition of the data structures used in your service communication.

Creating a .proto File

To define a gRPC service with Protocol Buffers, you create a file with the .proto extension. This file contains:

- Message Definitions: These define the structure of the data that will be exchanged between the client and the server. Each message is like a small data structure, containing fields with specific data types (integers, strings, booleans, etc.).[2]
- Service Definition: This defines the methods that the server will expose to clients. Each method specifies the request message it accepts and the response message it returns.

Example: Defining an "Inventory" Service

Let's say you're building an e-commerce application, and you need a service to manage product inventory. You could define a gRPC service called InventoryService with the following .proto file:

Protocol Buffers

```
syntax = "proto3";

package inventory;

// The inventory service definition.

service InventoryService {

  // Gets the current inventory level for a
product.

  rpc GetProductQuantity
(GetProductQuantityRequest) returns
(GetProductQuantityResponse) {}

  // Updates the inventory level for a product.

  rpc UpdateProductQuantity
(UpdateProductQuantityRequest) returns
(UpdateProductQuantityResponse) {}

}

// Request message for GetProductQuantity.

message GetProductQuantityRequest {

  int32 product_id = 1;

}

// Response message for GetProductQuantity.

message GetProductQuantityResponse {

  int32 quantity = 1;

}
```

```
// Request message for UpdateProductQuantity.

message UpdateProductQuantityRequest {

  int32 product_id = 1;

  int32 quantity_change = 2;

}

// Response message for UpdateProductQuantity.

message UpdateProductQuantityResponse {

  bool success = 1;

}
```

In this .proto file:

- We define a service called InventoryService with two methods: GetProductQuantity and UpdateProductQuantity.
- The GetProductQuantity method takes a GetProductQuantityRequest message (containing the product_id) as input and returns a GetProductQuantityResponse message (containing the quantity).
- The UpdateProductQuantity method takes an UpdateProductQuantityRequest message (containing the product_id and quantity_change) and returns an UpdateProductQuantityResponse message (indicating whether the update was successful).
- We define the structure of each message, specifying the data types and field numbers.[3]

Field Numbers in Protobuf

You'll notice that each field in a protobuf message has a number (e.g., product_id = 1). These field numbers are important for efficient encoding and backward compatibility. Make sure to choose field numbers carefully and avoid reusing them within the same message.

Benefits of Using Protocol Buffers

- Efficiency: Protobuf's binary encoding format is more compact and efficient than JSON or XML, resulting in smaller message sizes and faster serialization/deserialization.[4]
- Clarity: Protobuf provides a clear and concise way to define data structures, making it easy to understand the format of messages exchanged between services.[5]
- Type Safety: Protobuf enforces type safety, ensuring that the data types of fields match the expected types.
- Language-Agnostic: Protobuf supports code generation for various programming languages, making it suitable for polyglot systems.[6]
- Backward Compatibility: Protobuf is designed for backward compatibility, allowing you to evolve your message definitions without breaking existing clients.[7]

Real-World Examples

Protocol Buffers are used in various applications:

- gRPC: gRPC uses protobuf as its default data format for efficient communication.[8]
- API Design: Some APIs use protobuf as an alternative to JSON for data exchange.[9]
- Data Storage: Protobuf can be used to serialize data for storage in files or databases.

8.3 Building gRPC Clients and Servers

You've defined your gRPC service and its data structures using Protocol Buffers. Now, let's bring that service to life by building a gRPC server and a client that can interact with it. This is where the rubber meets the road – we'll write the actual Go code that handles requests, performs actions, and exchanges data using gRPC.

Think of it like this: you have the blueprint for a robot (the .proto file). Now, you need to assemble the robot (the server), write the instructions that control its actions (the server logic), and create a remote control (the client) to interact with it.

Generating Go Code from Protobuf

Before you can start writing your server and client code, you need to generate Go code from your .proto file. This generated code provides the data structures and gRPC service definitions that you'll use in your Go programs.

To generate Go code, you use the protoc compiler with the Go plugin. Here's an example of how to generate Go code from a file named inventory.proto:

```Bash
protoc --go_out=. --go_opt=paths=source_relative \

    --go-grpc_out=.
--go-grpc_opt=paths=source_relative \

    inventory.proto
```

This command generates two Go files:

- inventory.pb.go: Contains the message definitions (like GetProductQuantityRequest and GetProductQuantityResponse) from your .proto file.
- inventory_grpc.pb.go: Contains the gRPC service definitions (like the InventoryService interface) from your .proto file.

Building the gRPC Server

Now, let's build the gRPC server. This involves implementing the service interface defined in your .proto file and starting a gRPC server that listens for incoming requests.

Here's an example of a Go server that implements the InventoryService from our previous example:

```go
Go

package main

import (

    "context"

    "fmt"

    "log"

    "net"

    "google.golang.org/grpc"

    pb "your-module-path/inventory" // Replace
with the actual path to your generated protobuf
code

)
```

```go
// server is used to implement
helloworld.GreeterServer.

type server struct {

    pb.UnimplementedInventoryServiceServer

}

// GetProductQuantity implements the
GetProductQuantity method of the
InventoryService.

func (s *server) GetProductQuantity(ctx
context.Context, in
*pb.GetProductQuantityRequest)
(*pb.GetProductQuantityResponse, error) {

    log.Printf("Received: %v",
in.GetProductId())

    // ... (Logic to fetch quantity from the
database) ...

    return
&pb.GetProductQuantityResponse{Quantity: 123},
nil // Replace with actual quantity

}

// UpdateProductQuantity implements the
UpdateProductQuantity method of the
InventoryService.

func (s *server) UpdateProductQuantity(ctx
context.Context, in
*pb.UpdateProductQuantityRequest)
(*pb.UpdateProductQuantityResponse, error) {
```

```go
    log.Printf("Received: %v", in)

    // ... (Logic to update quantity in the
database) ...

    return
&pb.UpdateProductQuantityResponse{Success: true},
nil // Replace with actual success status

}

func main() {

    lis, err := net.Listen("tcp", ":50051") //
Listen on port 50051

    if err != nil {

        log.Fatalf("failed to listen: %v", err)

    }

    s := grpc.NewServer()

    pb.RegisterInventoryServiceServer(s,
&server{}) // Register the server

    log.Printf("server listening at %v",
lis.Addr())

    if err := s.Serve(lis); err != nil {

        log.Fatalf("failed to serve: %v", err)

    }

}
```

In this code:

- We create a server struct that implements the InventoryService interface.
- We implement the GetProductQuantity and UpdateProductQuantity methods, adding the logic to interact with the database (represented here by placeholders).
- We create a gRPC server and register our server with it.
- We start the server to listen for incoming requests on port 50051.

Building the gRPC Client

Now, let's build a gRPC client that can communicate with the server. The client will use the generated Go code to create a client stub and call the server's methods.

```Go
package main

import (

    "context"

    "fmt"

    "log"

    "os"

    "time"

    "google.golang.org/grpc"

    pb "your-module-path/inventory" // Replace
with the actual path to your generated protobuf
code

)
```

```go
func main() {

    // Set up a connection to the server.

    conn, err := grpc.Dial("localhost:50051",
grpc.WithInsecure())

    if err != nil {

        log.Fatalf("did not connect: %v", err)

    }

    defer conn.Close()

    c := pb.NewInventoryServiceClient(conn)

    // Get product quantity

    ctx, cancel :=
context.WithTimeout(context.Background(),
time.Second)

    defer cancel()

    r, err := c.GetProductQuantity(ctx,
&pb.GetProductQuantityRequest{ProductId: 123})

    if err != nil {

        log.Fatalf("could not get product
quantity: %v", err)

    }

    log.Printf("Product quantity: %d",
r.GetQuantity())

    // Update product quantity
```

```go
    ctx, cancel =
context.WithTimeout(context.Background(),
time.Second)

    defer cancel()

    r2, err := c.UpdateProductQuantity(ctx,
&pb.UpdateProductQuantityRequest{ProductId: 123,
QuantityChange: 10})

    if err != nil {

        log.Fatalf("could not update product
quantity: %v", err)

    }

    log.Printf("Update successful: %t",
r2.GetSuccess())

}
```

In this code:

- We create a gRPC connection to the server.
- We create a client stub for the InventoryService.
- We call the GetProductQuantity and UpdateProductQuantity methods on the server, passing the necessary request messages.
- We handle the responses from the server.

Real-World Examples

gRPC is used in various real-world applications:

- Cloud-Native Applications: Many cloud-native applications use gRPC for efficient communication between microservices.

- Streaming Services: Streaming services like Netflix and Spotify use gRPC for real-time communication and data streaming.
- Financial Systems: Financial institutions use gRPC for high-performance communication in trading systems and other critical applications.

8.4 gRPC in a Microservices Architecture

Let's discuss how gRPC fits into the world of microservices. As you know, in a microservices architecture, you break down your application into smaller, independent services that communicate with each other. This inter-service communication is crucial, and gRPC offers a compelling approach, especially when performance, efficiency, and type safety are paramount.

Think of a bustling city with various districts (microservices) that need to interact and exchange goods and services. gRPC is like building a high-speed rail network between those districts, enabling fast and efficient transportation.

Why gRPC for Microservices?

gRPC offers several advantages that make it well-suited for communication within a microservices architecture:

- Performance: gRPC's use of Protocol Buffers and HTTP/2 results in significantly faster communication compared to traditional RESTful APIs with JSON. This is crucial in microservices, where services often need to communicate with each other frequently.
- Efficiency: Protobuf's compact binary format reduces the size of messages, leading to less data being transmitted over the network and faster serialization/deserialization. This

efficiency is essential for optimizing resource utilization and minimizing latency in microservices.

- Type Safety: gRPC's contract-first approach with Protocol Buffers ensures type safety, meaning that the client and server have a shared understanding of the data types being exchanged. This reduces errors caused by data type mismatches, which can be common in systems that use loosely typed formats like JSON.
- Streaming: gRPC supports various streaming capabilities, allowing services to send and receive streams of messages. This is useful for scenarios like real-time updates, chat applications, or large data transfers between microservices.
- Language-Agnostic: gRPC supports a wide range of programming languages. This is important in microservices, where different services might be written in different languages based on their specific needs and the strengths of different technologies.

Example: Microservices Communication with gRPC

Consider an e-commerce application with separate microservices for product catalog, order management, and user accounts. These services might use gRPC to communicate with each other:

- **Order Management Service:** When a user places an order, the Order Management Service might use gRPC to call the Product Catalog Service to:
  - Get product details (name, description, price) for the items in the order.
  - Update the inventory levels of those products.
- **User Accounts Service:** The User Accounts Service might use gRPC to:
  - Authenticate users when they log in.
  - Retrieve user profile information.
  - Send notifications to users about their orders or account activity.

Benefits of Using gRPC in Microservices

- Improved Performance: gRPC's efficiency leads to faster communication and reduced latency between microservices, improving the overall performance of the application.
- Reduced Errors: Type safety and clear contracts with Protocol Buffers reduce the risk of errors due to data type mismatches or API changes.
- Increased Scalability: gRPC's performance and efficiency make it easier to scale microservices independently, as they can handle more requests with fewer resources.
- Simplified Development: The contract-first approach and code generation features of gRPC can simplify development by providing clear interfaces and reducing boilerplate code.

Real-World Examples

Many companies use gRPC in their microservices architectures:

- Netflix: Uses gRPC extensively for communication between its microservices, handling millions of streaming requests and ensuring a smooth user experience.
- Uber: Relies on gRPC for efficient communication between its various services, such as ride dispatching, payment processing, and location tracking.
- Square: Uses gRPC for communication between its point-of-sale systems, payment processing services, and other backend systems.

Considerations for Using gRPC

While gRPC offers many advantages, there are also some considerations:

- Browser Support: gRPC is not as directly compatible with web browsers as RESTful APIs, which might require using proxies or gateways for browser-based communication.
- Learning Curve: gRPC has a slightly steeper learning curve compared to REST, as it involves learning Protocol Buffers and the gRPC framework.
- Monitoring and Debugging: Monitoring and debugging gRPC communication can be more challenging than REST, requiring specialized tools and techniques.

By carefully considering these factors and understanding the strengths of gRPC, you can make informed decisions about when and how to use it in your microservices architecture.

Chapter 9: Security Best Practices

Security is paramount when building any application, especially backend systems that handle sensitive data and critical operations. In this chapter, we'll discuss essential security best practices for your Go applications, covering authentication and authorization, common vulnerabilities, secure coding practices, and security in a cloud environment. Think of this as fortifying your application against potential attacks and vulnerabilities, ensuring that your data and users are protected.

9.1 Authentication and Authorization

Let's talk about two fundamental pillars of security in web applications: authentication and authorization. These are essential for protecting your application and its users, ensuring that only authorized individuals can access sensitive data and perform specific actions.

Think of it like entering a secure building. Authentication is like showing your ID card to the security guard at the entrance to prove your identity. Authorization is like the guard checking your ID against a list to see which rooms or floors you're allowed to access.

Authentication

Authentication is the process of verifying the identity of a user or service. It's about confirming that someone or something is who they claim to be. In web applications, authentication is typically used to control access to protected resources or functionalities.

Here are some common authentication methods:

- Passwords: This is the most traditional method, where users provide a username and password, which are then compared against stored credentials (usually hashed and salted for security).

- API Keys: API keys are secret keys that clients use to authenticate their requests to an API. This is often used for server-to-server communication or for allowing external applications to access your API.
- Tokens: Tokens, such as JWTs (JSON Web Tokens), are often used for authentication in modern web applications. After a user successfully authenticates (e.g., with a username/password), the server issues a token that the user can use to authorize subsequent requests. This token contains information about the user's identity and permissions.
- Multi-Factor Authentication (MFA): MFA adds an extra layer of security by requiring users to provide multiple factors for authentication. This might involve something they know (password), something they have (a one-time code sent to their phone), or something they are (biometric authentication).
- OAuth 2.0: OAuth 2.0 is an authorization framework that allows users to grant third-party applications access to their resources without sharing their credentials.[1] This is commonly used for social logins (e.g., "Login with Google") or for allowing applications to access user data on other platforms.

Authorization

Once a user or service is authenticated, authorization determines what actions they are allowed to perform. This involves checking their role, permissions, or other attributes to ensure they have the necessary privileges.

Common authorization mechanisms include:

- Role-Based Access Control (RBAC): RBAC assigns users to roles (e.g., admin, editor, viewer) with specific permissions.

This simplifies authorization by grouping users with similar access needs.

- Attribute-Based Access Control (ABAC): ABAC defines access based on attributes of users, resources, and the environment. This provides more fine-grained control over authorization, allowing you to define complex access rules based on various factors.

Example: Implementing JWT Authentication in Go

Here's an example of how you might implement JWT (JSON Web Token) authentication in a Go web application:

```go
Go

package main

import (

    "fmt"

    "net/http"

    "time"

    "github.com/dgrijalva/jwt-go"

)

// Define a secret key for signing JWTs

var jwtKey = []byte("your_secret_key") // Replace
with a strong, randomly generated key

// Create a struct to represent the JWT claims

type Claims struct {

    Username string `json:"username"`
```

```go
        jwt.StandardClaims

}

func generateJWT(username string) (string, error)
{

        expirationTime := time.Now().Add(15 *
time.Minute)

        claims := &Claims{

                Username: username,

                StandardClaims: jwt.StandardClaims{

                        ExpiresAt: expirationTime.Unix(),

                },

        }

        token :=
jwt.NewWithClaims(jwt.SigningMethodHS256, claims)

        tokenString, err :=
token.SignedString(jwtKey)

        if err != nil {

                return "", fmt.Errorf("failed to
generate JWT: %w", err)

        }

        return tokenString, nil

}

func main() {
```

```go
    // ... (Your HTTP server logic) ...

    http.HandleFunc("/login", func(w
http.ResponseWriter, r *http.Request) {

        // ... (Authenticate the user, e.g.,
check username and password) ...

        tokenString, err :=
generateJWT("testuser") // Generate JWT for
authenticated user

        if err != nil {

            http.Error(w, "Failed to generate
JWT", http.StatusInternalServerError)

            return

        }

        w.Write([]byte(tokenString)) // Send
the JWT to the client

    })

}
```

In this code:

- We define a secret key (jwtKey) for signing JWTs. This key should be kept confidential.
- We define a Claims struct to represent the data that will be encoded in the JWT.
- The generateJWT function creates a JWT with the user's username and an expiration time.
- In the /login handler, we authenticate the user and then generate a JWT for them.

You would then use middleware to validate the JWT in subsequent requests and authorize the user based on the claims in the JWT.

Real-World Examples

Authentication and authorization are used in almost every web application:

- Online Banking: Banks use strong authentication (like MFA) and authorization to protect user accounts and financial transactions.
- E-commerce: Online stores use authentication to manage user accounts and authorization to control access to order history, payment information, and other sensitive data.
- Social Media: Social media platforms use authentication to identify users and authorization to control who can view their profiles, posts, and other content.

9.2 Protecting Against Common Vulnerabilities

Building secure applications requires a proactive approach to identifying and mitigating potential vulnerabilities. Think of it like securing your home – you wouldn't just leave the doors and windows unlocked, would you? You would take measures like installing locks, reinforcing windows, and maybe even setting up an alarm system to protect against potential intruders.

Similarly, web applications are susceptible to various security vulnerabilities that attackers can exploit to gain unauthorized access, steal data, or disrupt your services. Let's discuss some common web application vulnerabilities and how to protect against them in your Go applications.

1. SQL Injection

SQL injection is a type of attack where malicious SQL code is inserted into your application's database queries. This can allow attackers to manipulate your database, steal data, or even take control of your server.

How to Prevent SQL Injection:

- Use Parameterized Queries or Prepared Statements: Instead of constructing SQL queries by concatenating strings, use parameterized queries or prepared statements. These techniques treat user input as data rather than executable code, preventing attackers from injecting malicious SQL.

Example (using database/sql **package):**

```Go
// Vulnerable code (concatenating strings)

name := r.FormValue("name")

query := "SELECT * FROM users WHERE name = '" +
name + "'"

rows, err := db.Query(query)

// Secure code (using parameterized query)

name := r.FormValue("name")

rows, err := db.Query("SELECT * FROM users WHERE
name = ?", name)
```

In the secure code, the ? acts as a placeholder for the name parameter, and the database driver handles escaping the input correctly to prevent SQL injection.

2. Cross-Site Scripting (XSS)

XSS attacks involve injecting malicious scripts into web pages viewed by other users. These scripts can[1] then steal user data, hijack sessions, or redirect users to malicious websites.

How to Prevent XSS:

- Escape User Input: Always escape user input before displaying it on web pages. This converts special characters (like <, >, and ") into their HTML entity equivalents, preventing them from being interpreted as code.

Example (using html/template package):

```Go
// Vulnerable code (not escaping user input)

tmpl :=
template.Must(template.New("name").Parse("<h1>Hel
lo, {{.Name}}!</h1>"))

tmpl.Execute(w, data)

// Secure code (escaping user input)

tmpl :=
template.Must(template.New("name").Parse("<h1>Hel
lo, {{.Name | html}}!</h1>"))

tmpl.Execute(w, data)
```

In the secure code, the html template function escapes the Name variable before rendering it, preventing any malicious scripts from being executed.

3. Cross-Site Request Forgery (CSRF)

CSRF attacks trick users into performing unwanted actions on your website. This is often done by including malicious links or forms in emails or other websites that, when clicked, trigger actions on your site without the user's knowledge.

How to Prevent CSRF:

- Use CSRF Tokens: Generate unique, unpredictable tokens for each user session and include them in forms. When a form is submitted, verify that the token matches the one stored in the user's session. This prevents attackers from forging requests.

Example (using Gorilla CSRF package):

```Go
import "github.com/gorilla/csrf"

// ... (Your HTTP server logic) ...

// Configure CSRF protection

var csrfMiddleware =
csrf.Protect([]byte("your_csrf_secret"),

    csrf.Secure(true), // Set to false for
development environments

)

// Apply CSRF middleware to your routes

http.Handle("/protected",
csrfMiddleware(protectedHandler))
```

The Gorilla CSRF package provides middleware that generates and validates CSRF tokens.

4. Denial of Service (DoS)

DoS attacks aim to overwhelm your server with traffic, making it unavailable to legitimate users.

How to Mitigate DoS Attacks:

- Rate Limiting: Limit the number of requests a user or IP address can make within a certain time frame.
- Traffic Filtering: Use firewalls and other network security measures to block malicious traffic.
- Use a CDN: A CDN can absorb some of the traffic and protect your origin server.
- Cloud Provider DDoS Protection: Leverage DDoS protection services offered by your cloud provider.

5. Sensitive Data Exposure

Sensitive data like passwords, credit card information, and API keys should be protected both in transit and at rest.

How to Protect Sensitive Data:

- Encryption: Encrypt data in transit using HTTPS and encrypt data at rest using encryption algorithms.
- Secure Storage: Store sensitive data securely, such as in encrypted databases or secure vaults.
- Follow Security Best Practices: Adhere to industry best practices for handling sensitive data, such as PCI DSS for payment card information.

Real-World Examples

These vulnerabilities have been exploited in real-world attacks:

- SQL Injection: A SQL injection vulnerability in a popular forum software allowed attackers to steal millions of user accounts.

- XSS: An XSS vulnerability in a social media platform allowed attackers to spread malicious links and steal user data.
- CSRF: A CSRF vulnerability in a webmail service allowed attackers to send emails from users' accounts without their knowledge.

9.3 Secure Coding Practices

Writing secure code isn't just about patching vulnerabilities after they appear; it's about adopting a security-conscious mindset from the very beginning.[1] Think of it like building a house with strong foundations and sturdy materials – it's much easier to prevent problems than to fix them later.

Secure coding practices are a set of guidelines and habits that help you write code that is inherently more resistant to attacks and vulnerabilities.[2] These practices are essential for building robust and trustworthy Go applications.[3]

1. Validate Input

One of the most fundamental principles of secure coding is to never trust user input. Always validate and sanitize any data that comes from external sources, such as user forms, API requests, or file uploads.

- Validate Data Types and Formats: Ensure that the input data matches the expected data type (e.g., integer, string, email address) and format.[4]
- Check for Length and Range: Validate the length of strings and the range of numerical values to prevent buffer overflows or other issues.[5]

- Sanitize Input: Remove or escape potentially harmful characters that could be used for injection attacks (like SQL injection or XSS).[6]

Example: Validating User Input

```go
Go

package main

import (

    "fmt"

    "net/http"

    "regexp"

)

func handler(w http.ResponseWriter, r *http.Request) {

    name := r.FormValue("name")

    email := r.FormValue("email")

    // Validate name (must not be empty)

    if name == "" {

        http.Error(w, "Name is required", http.StatusBadRequest)

        return

    }

    // Validate email format
```

```
    emailRegex :=
regexp.MustCompile(`^[a-zA-Z0-9._%+-]+@[a-zA-Z0-9
.-]+\.[a-zA-Z]{2,}$`)

    if !emailRegex.MatchString(email) {

        http.Error(w, "Invalid email format",
http.StatusBadRequest)

        return

    }

    // ... process the validated input ...

}
```

In this code, we validate that the name field is not empty and that the email field matches a regular expression for valid email formats.

2. Principle of Least Privilege

Grant users and services only the necessary permissions they need to perform their tasks.[7] Avoid granting excessive privileges that could be exploited if an account is compromised.[8]

- User Roles and Permissions: Implement role-based access control (RBAC) to assign users to roles with specific permissions.
- Service Accounts: Use service accounts with limited permissions for automated tasks and integrations.[9]

3. Keep Dependencies Updated

Open-source libraries and frameworks are often used in Go applications. These dependencies might contain security vulnerabilities that can be exploited by attackers.

- Regularly Update Dependencies: Use tools like go get -u or dependency management tools (like dep or go mod) to update your dependencies to the latest versions, which often include security patches.
- Use Vulnerability Scanners: Use vulnerability scanners (like gosec or govulncheck) to identify known vulnerabilities in your dependencies.

4. Securely Store Sensitive Data

Protect sensitive data like passwords, API keys, and credit card information by:

- Hashing and Salting Passwords: Never store passwords in plain text.[10] Use strong hashing algorithms (like bcrypt or Argon2) and salt the passwords to make them more resistant to cracking.
- Encrypting Data: Encrypt sensitive data at rest and in transit using encryption algorithms and secure storage solutions.[11]
- Following Industry Best Practices: Adhere to industry-specific security standards like PCI DSS for handling payment card information.

5. Use Security Linters

Security linters are tools that analyze your code to identify potential security vulnerabilities and insecure coding practices.[12]

- gosec: A popular security linter for Go that can detect issues like SQL injection, XSS, and insecure use of cryptography.[13]
- govulncheck: A tool that checks your code for known vulnerabilities in your dependencies.[14]

6. Code Reviews

Code reviews are an essential part of secure coding practices. Having other developers review your code can help identify potential security issues that you might have missed.

7. Security Training

Keep your development team informed about security best practices and emerging threats through regular security training and awareness programs.[15]

Real-World Examples

Secure coding practices are essential for building trustworthy applications:

- Financial Institutions: Banks and other financial institutions rely on secure coding practices to protect customer data and financial transactions.[16]
- Healthcare: Healthcare applications must adhere to strict security regulations (like HIPAA) to protect patient data.[17]
- Government: Government systems often handle sensitive information and require secure coding practices to prevent data breaches.[18]

9.4 Security in a Cloud Environment

Moving your Go applications to the cloud offers many benefits, like scalability and flexibility.[1] However, it also introduces new security considerations.[2] Think of it like moving from a standalone house to an apartment building. While the apartment building might have security features like a doorman and security cameras, you still need to take precautions to protect your own apartment, like locking your door and being mindful of who you let in.

Similarly, cloud providers offer security measures to protect their infrastructure, but you are ultimately responsible for securing your own applications and data within the cloud environment.[3]

Let's discuss some essential security best practices for deploying and running your Go applications in the cloud.

1. Secure Your Cloud Accounts

Your cloud account is the gateway to your cloud resources.[4] Protect it like you would protect your most valuable possessions.

- Strong Passwords and MFA: Use strong, unique passwords for your cloud accounts and enable multi-factor authentication (MFA) whenever possible.[5] MFA adds an extra layer of security by requiring a second form of verification, such as a code sent to your phone or a biometric scan.[7]
- Principle of Least Privilege: Follow the principle of least privilege by granting users and services only the necessary permissions they need to perform their tasks.[89] Avoid creating overly powerful accounts or roles that could be exploited if compromised.
- Regularly Review and Revoke Credentials: Periodically review the users and permissions associated with your cloud accounts and revoke any unnecessary access.

2. Network Security

Cloud providers offer various network security features to control access to your resources.[10]

- Firewalls: Use firewalls to restrict incoming and outgoing traffic to your cloud resources.[11] Configure firewall rules to allow only necessary traffic and block any unwanted connections.[12]
- Security Groups: Security groups act like virtual firewalls for your cloud instances (like EC2 instances on AWS or Virtual Machines on Azure).[13] Configure security groups to control inbound and outbound traffic to your instances, allowing only necessary ports and protocols.[14]
- Virtual Private Cloud (VPC): VPCs allow you to create isolated networks within the cloud provider's

infrastructure.[15] You can use VPCs to segment your applications and control network access between different components.[16]

3. Data Security

Protecting your data in the cloud is crucial. Cloud providers offer various tools and services to help you secure your data.[17]

- Encryption at Rest: Encrypt your data at rest, meaning when it's stored in databases, storage buckets, or other cloud services.[18] Most cloud providers offer encryption services that can automatically encrypt your data without requiring code changes.
- Encryption in Transit: Encrypt data in transit, meaning when it's being transmitted between your application and other services or users.[19] Use HTTPS for all web traffic and encrypt any sensitive data that is sent over the network.
- Access Control: Use access control mechanisms (like IAM - Identity and Access Management) to restrict access to your data and resources.[20] Grant permissions only to authorized users and services.
- Data Loss Prevention (DLP): Consider using DLP tools to prevent sensitive data from leaving your cloud environment.[21] These tools can identify and block attempts to send sensitive data outside your organization.[22]

4. Monitoring and Logging

Monitoring and logging are essential for detecting and responding to security incidents in the cloud.[23]

- Security Information and Event Management (SIEM): Use SIEM tools to collect and analyze security logs from various sources, including your cloud provider, applications, and security devices.[24] SIEM tools can help you identify suspicious activity and potential threats.[25]

- Intrusion Detection and Prevention Systems (IDPS): Consider using IDPS to monitor network traffic for malicious activity and block attacks.[26]
- Cloud Provider Security Tools: Leverage security tools and services offered by your cloud provider.[27] These might include security information dashboards, vulnerability scanners, and threat intelligence feeds.

5. Secure Configuration Management

Misconfigured cloud resources can lead to security vulnerabilities.[28]

- Infrastructure as Code (IaC): Use IaC tools (like Terraform or CloudFormation) to define and manage your cloud infrastructure in a declarative way.[29] This helps ensure consistent and secure configurations.
- Configuration Monitoring: Use tools to monitor your cloud configurations for changes and ensure they comply with security best practices.[30]

Real-World Examples

- Capital One: A misconfigured web application firewall led to a data breach that exposed the personal information of millions of customers.[31]
- Code Spaces: A vulnerability in GitHub's Code Spaces feature allowed attackers to gain access to user repositories.

These examples highlight the importance of security in a cloud environment. By following these best practices, you can mitigate risks, protect your applications and data, and build secure and reliable systems in the cloud.

Chapter 10: Testing and Continuous Integration

Testing and continuous integration (CI) are essential practices for building high-quality and reliable Go applications. Think of it like this: you wouldn't build a bridge without thoroughly testing each component and ensuring that they fit together seamlessly, would you? Similarly, testing your code helps you catch errors early, and CI helps you integrate code changes smoothly and ensure that your application remains in a working state.

In this chapter, we'll explore different types of testing, learn about testing frameworks and tools, and see how to implement CI for your Go projects. We'll also touch on continuous delivery (CD), which takes CI a step further by automating the deployment process.

10.1 Types of Testing

Testing is a crucial aspect of software development, especially when building backend systems with Go. It helps you ensure that your code works correctly, catches errors early, and gives you confidence in the reliability of your application. Think of it like building a car. You wouldn't just assemble all the parts and hope for the best, would you? You would test each component individually, then test how they work together, and finally take the car for a test drive to make sure everything functions as expected.

Similarly, testing your Go applications involves different levels of testing, each with its own focus and scope: unit testing, integration testing, and end-to-end testing. Let's explore each of these in detail.

1. Unit Testing

Unit tests focus on testing the smallest units of your code, typically individual functions or methods, in isolation. They help you verify that each unit behaves correctly on its own, independent of other parts of the system.

Think of it like testing the individual components of a car – the engine, the brakes, the transmission – in a controlled environment to ensure they function correctly before assembling the whole car.

Benefits of Unit Testing:

- Early Error Detection: Unit tests help you catch errors early in the development process, when they are easier and cheaper to fix.
- Improved Code Design: Writing unit tests encourages you to design your code in a modular and testable way, leading to better code organization and maintainability.
- Facilitates Refactoring: When you have a comprehensive suite of unit tests, you can confidently refactor your code, knowing that the tests will catch any regressions or unintended side effects.
- Documentation: Well-written unit tests can serve as documentation, demonstrating how individual units of code are intended to be used.

Example: Unit Testing a Function in Go

```Go
package mypackage

import "testing"

// Function to be tested

func calculateDiscount(price float64,
discountPercentage int) float64 {
```

```go
    discount := price *
(float64(discountPercentage) / 100)

    return price - discount

}

// Unit test for the calculateDiscount function

func TestCalculateDiscount(t *testing.T) {

    testCases := []struct {

        price               float64

        discountPercentage int

        expectedDiscount   float64

    }{

        {100, 10, 90},

        {50, 20, 40},

        {200, 5, 190},

    }

    for _, tc := range testCases {

        t.Run(fmt.Sprintf("Price %.2f, Discount
%d%%", tc.price, tc.discountPercentage), func(t
*testing.T) {

            actualDiscount :=
calculateDiscount(tc.price,
tc.discountPercentage)

            if actualDiscount != tc.expectedDiscount {
```

```
        t.Errorf("Expected discount: %.2f, got:
%.2f", tc.expectedDiscount, actualDiscount)

    }

  })

 }

}
```

In this example:

- We define a function calculateDiscount that calculates the discounted price of an item.
- We write a unit test TestCalculateDiscount that defines several test cases with different input values and expected outputs.
- The test function iterates through the test cases and checks if the actual output of calculateDiscount matches the expected output.

2. Integration Testing: Testing the Connections

Integration tests focus on testing the interactions between different units of code or modules within your application. They verify that these components work together correctly and that data flows as expected between them.

Think of it like testing how different parts of a car interact – does the engine transmit power to the wheels correctly? Do the brakes work effectively to stop the car?

Benefits of Integration Testing:

- Catch Integration Errors: Integration tests help you identify errors that might arise from the interaction between different components, such as data inconsistencies, communication problems, or unexpected side effects.

- Ensure System Functionality: They verify that different parts of your application work together correctly to achieve the desired functionality.
- Increase Confidence: Integration tests provide a higher level of confidence in the overall system's behavior compared to unit tests alone.

Example Scenario: Integration Testing a User Registration Flow

Let's say you have a user registration flow that involves:

- A web form to collect user data.
- An API endpoint to handle the registration request.
- A database to store user information.

An integration test for this flow might involve:

- Simulating a user submitting the registration form.
- Verifying that the API endpoint receives the data correctly.
- Checking that the user data is stored correctly in the database.

3. End-to-End (E2E) Testing

End-to-end (E2E) tests take a broader perspective, testing the entire application from start to finish, simulating real user scenarios. They help you ensure that the application behaves as expected from the user's point of view.

Think of it like taking the car for a test drive on a real road, with a real driver, to make sure all the parts work together seamlessly and provide a smooth driving experience.

Benefits of E2E Testing:

- Catch System-Level Errors: E2E tests can uncover errors that might not be apparent in unit or integration tests, such as issues with user interface interactions, external dependencies, or overall system behavior.

- Ensure User Flows Work Correctly: They verify that users can successfully complete critical flows within your application, such as registering an account, placing an order, or making a payment.
- Increase User Confidence: E2E tests provide a high level of confidence that the application works as expected for real users.

Example Scenario: E2E Testing an E-commerce Checkout Flow

An E2E test for an e-commerce checkout flow might involve:

- Simulating a user browsing products, adding them to their cart, and proceeding to checkout.
- Entering shipping and payment information.
- Completing the order and verifying that the order confirmation is displayed.

Real-World Examples

These different levels of testing are used in various real-world applications:

- Web Applications: Unit tests for individual functions, integration tests for API endpoints and database interactions, and E2E tests for user flows like registration and checkout.
- Microservices: Unit tests for individual services, integration tests for communication between services, and E2E tests for the overall system behavior.
- Mobile Applications: Unit tests for individual components, integration tests for interactions with backend APIs, and E2E tests for user interactions within the app.

10.2 Testing Frameworks and Tools

While Go provides a built-in testing framework with the testing package, it can sometimes feel a bit basic, especially when dealing with complex assertions or mocking dependencies. Thankfully, the Go ecosystem offers a variety of third-party testing frameworks and tools that can enhance your testing experience and make your tests more expressive, maintainable, and robust.

Think of it like this: you have a basic set of tools for woodworking, but specialized tools like a power drill or a jigsaw can make your work more efficient and precise. Similarly, these testing frameworks and tools provide specialized functionalities to improve your testing workflow.

1. Testify/assert

Testify is a popular testing framework for Go that provides a comprehensive set of assertion functions.[1] These functions allow you to express your test expectations in a more readable and concise way, making your test code easier to understand and maintain.

Instead of writing verbose if statements to check conditions, you can use Testify's assertion functions like:

- assert.Equal(t, expected, actual): Checks if two values are equal.
- assert.NotEqual(t, expected, actual): Checks if two values are not equal.
- assert.True(t, condition): Checks if a condition is true.
- assert.False(t, condition): Checks if a condition is false.
- assert.Nil(t, object): Checks if an object is nil.
- assert.NotNil(t, object): Checks if an object is not nil.

Example: Using Testify/assert

Go

```go
package mypackage

import (

    "testing"

    "github.com/stretchr/testify/assert"

)

func TestCalculateDiscount(t *testing.T) {

    price := 100.0

    discountPercentage := 10

    expectedDiscount := 90.0

    actualDiscount := calculateDiscount(price,
discountPercentage)

    assert.Equal(t, expectedDiscount,
actualDiscount, "Discount calculation is
incorrect")

}
```

In this example, we use assert.Equal to check if the calculated discount matches the expected discount. If the assertion fails, the test will fail with a clear error message.

2. GoMock

GoMock is a mocking framework for Go that allows you to create mock objects for unit testing.[2] Mocking is a technique where you replace real dependencies with mock objects that simulate the behavior of those dependencies.[3] This allows you to isolate the unit under test and control its interactions with other parts of the system.

GoMock helps you:

- Define mock interfaces: You define interfaces for your dependencies.
- Generate mock implementations: GoMock generates mock implementations of those interfaces.[4]
- Set expectations: You define expectations on the mock objects, specifying how they should behave during the test.
- Verify interactions: GoMock verifies that the unit under test interacted with the mock objects as expected.

Example Scenario: Using GoMock to Mock a Database

Let's say you have a function that retrieves user data from a database. In a unit test, you might want to mock the database interaction to avoid relying on a real database connection.

You would define an interface for your database interactions:

```Go
type UserDB interface {

  GetUser(userID int) (User, error)

}
```

Then, you would use GoMock to generate a mock implementation of this interface:[5]

```Bash
mockgen -source=user_db.go
-destination=mock_user_db.go -package=mypackage
```

This generates a mock_user_db.go file with a mock implementation of the UserDB interface. You can then use this mock object in your unit tests to simulate database interactions and control the data returned.

3. Httpmock

Httpmock is a library that allows you to mock HTTP requests for testing.[6] This is useful when your Go application interacts with external APIs or services. Httpmock allows you to:

- Mock HTTP responses: You can define mock responses for specific HTTP requests, simulating different scenarios like successful responses, error responses, or specific response bodies.[7]
- Test error handling: You can simulate network errors or API failures to test how your application handles these situations.[8]
- Avoid external dependencies: You can avoid relying on external APIs during testing, making your tests faster and more reliable.

Example: Using Httpmock to Mock an API Call

```Go
package mypackage

import (

    "net/http"

    "testing"

    "github.com/jarcoal/httpmock"

)

func TestFetchUserData(t *testing.T) {
```

```
httpmock.Activate()

defer httpmock.DeactivateAndReset()

// Mock the API response

httpmock.RegisterResponder("GET",
"https://api.example.com/users/123",

    httpmock.NewStringResponder(200,
`{"id": 123, "name": "Test User"}`))

// Call the function that makes the API call

user, err := fetchUserData(123)

assert.NoError(t, err)

assert.Equal(t, 123, user.ID)

assert.Equal(t, "Test User", user.Name)
}
```

In this example, we use Httpmock to mock the response from an API call.[9] This allows us to test the fetchUserData function without actually making a real API request.

4. Testify/suite

Testify/suite provides a suite for organizing and running test cases.[10] It allows you to group related test cases into suites, set up common test fixtures, and define setup and teardown methods that run before and after each test or suite.[11]

Other Testing Tools

- go test: Go's built-in testing tool.[12]

- Race Detector: Go's built-in race detector can help you identify data races in your concurrent code.[13]
- Code Coverage Tools: Tools like go tool cover can help you measure how much of your code is covered by tests.

Real-World Examples

These testing frameworks and tools are used by many companies and projects:

- Docker: The Docker project uses GoMock for mocking dependencies in its unit tests.
- Kubernetes: The Kubernetes project uses Testify/assert for assertions and GoMock for mocking.
- Many Go Projects: Numerous Go projects use these frameworks and tools to improve their testing practices.

By utilizing these testing frameworks and tools, you can write more effective, maintainable, and robust tests for your Go applications, ensuring that your code is reliable and works as expected.

10.3 Implementing Continuous Integration

Continuous Integration (CI) is a practice that can significantly improve the quality and efficiency of your Go development process. CI is like having an automated assistant that constantly checks your code for errors and ensures that your application remains in a working state as you and your team make changes.

Think of it like this: you're building a complex Lego model with a team of friends. Instead of each person building their own section in isolation and hoping it all fits together in the end, you use a CI approach. Every time someone adds a new piece or modifies an existing one, you check if it fits correctly with the rest of the model.

This way, you catch any errors early on and avoid ending up with a jumbled mess.

What is Continuous Integration?

Continuous Integration (CI) is a development practice where developers integrate code changes into a shared repository frequently, usually multiple times a day. Each integration triggers an automated build and test process, helping to:

- Catch errors early: CI helps you identify and fix errors quickly, before they become bigger problems.
- Improve code quality: Regular testing and feedback encourage developers to write better code.
- Reduce integration problems: Frequent integration helps prevent integration conflicts and ensures that the codebase remains in a working state.
- Increase collaboration: CI promotes collaboration among developers by providing a shared view of the codebase and its status.

The CI Workflow

A typical CI workflow looks like this:

1. Code Changes: Developers make changes to the codebase, working on new features, bug fixes, or improvements.
2. Commit: Developers commit their code changes to a shared version control repository (like Git).
3. Build Trigger: The CI system (e.g., Jenkins, CircleCI, GitHub Actions) detects the code changes and triggers a new build.
4. Build: The CI system builds the application, compiling the code and resolving dependencies.
5. Testing: Automated tests (unit tests, integration tests, and potentially end-to-end tests) are run to verify the code changes.

6. Feedback: The CI system provides feedback to the developers about the build and test results, usually through email notifications, chat messages, or a web dashboard.

Benefits of Continuous Integration

- Reduced Risk: CI helps you catch errors early, reducing the risk of releasing buggy software.
- Faster Feedback: Developers receive immediate feedback on their code changes, allowing them to fix errors quickly.
- Improved Collaboration: CI promotes collaboration and communication among developers.
- Increased Confidence: CI provides confidence that the codebase is always in a working state.
- Faster Releases: CI helps you release software more frequently and reliably.

Implementing CI for Your Go Projects

Here's a general outline of how you can implement CI for your Go projects:

1. Choose a CI System: Select a CI system that meets your needs. Popular options include Jenkins, CircleCI, Travis CI, and GitHub Actions.
2. Configure the CI System: Configure the CI system to connect to your version control repository and set up build triggers. This usually involves creating a configuration file (e.g., Jenkinsfile, .circleci/config.yml) that defines the build and test steps.
3. Write Automated Tests: Write a comprehensive suite of automated tests (unit, integration, and potentially E2E) to verify your code.
4. Define the Build Process: Define the build process for your Go application, including steps like compiling the code, running tests, and packaging the application.

5. Set Up Notifications: Configure the CI system to send notifications to your team about build and test results.

Example: .github/workflows/go.yml **for GitHub Actions**

```yaml
YAML

name: Go

on:

  push:

    branches: [ main ]

  pull_request:

    branches: [ main ]

jobs:

  build:

    runs-on: ubuntu-latest

    steps:

    - uses: actions/checkout@v3

    - name: Set up Go

      uses: actions/setup-go@v3

      with:

        go-version: 1.19

    - name: Build

      run: go build -v ./...
```

```
- name: Test

    run: go test -v ./...
```

This configuration file defines a CI workflow for a Go project on GitHub Actions. It triggers a build and test process on every push or pull request to the main branch.

Real-World Examples

Many companies and projects use CI to improve their development process:

- Google: Google uses CI extensively for its internal projects and open-source projects like Kubernetes.
- Netflix: Netflix uses CI to build and test its microservices architecture.
- Facebook: Facebook uses CI to ensure the quality and stability of its social media platform.

By implementing CI for your Go projects, you can adopt a more robust and efficient development workflow, leading to higher-quality code and faster releases.

10.4 Continuous Delivery for Go Applications

Continuous Delivery (CD) is a practice that takes Continuous Integration (CI) a step further and automates the deployment process. If CI is like having an automated quality control system for your code, CD is like having an automated delivery service that takes your thoroughly tested and packaged application and deploys it to your users.

Think of it like this: you have a bakery that produces delicious cakes. CI ensures that the ingredients are fresh and the baking process is flawless. CD takes those perfectly baked cakes and automatically delivers them to your customers, fresh and ready to enjoy.

What is Continuous Delivery?

Continuous Delivery (CD) is a software development practice where code changes are automatically built, tested, and deployed to a production (or staging) environment. This automation allows you to release new features and updates to your users quickly and reliably, with minimal manual intervention.

The CD Workflow

A typical CD workflow builds upon the CI process:

1. CI Process: The CI process builds, tests, and packages your Go application. This ensures that the code is in a releasable state.
2. Deployment Pipeline: A CD pipeline orchestrates the deployment process. It defines a series of stages, such as:
   - Deploy to Staging: Deploy the application to a staging environment that closely resembles the production environment.
   - Run Acceptance Tests: Run automated acceptance tests in the staging environment to verify that the application meets the defined acceptance criteria.
   - Manual Approval (Optional): Include a manual approval step where someone (e.g., a product manager or QA engineer) can review the changes and approve the deployment to production.
   - Deploy to Production: Deploy the application to the production environment, making it available to users.
3. Monitoring and Rollback: Monitor the deployed application for performance and stability. If any issues are detected, you can quickly roll back to a previous version.

Benefits of Continuous Delivery

- Faster Releases: CD enables you to release new features and updates more frequently, responding quickly to user needs and market demands.
- Reduced Risk: Automated testing and deployment reduce the risk of human error and ensure that deployments are consistent and reliable.
- Improved Collaboration: CD promotes collaboration between developers, operations, and other stakeholders by providing a shared view of the release process.
- Increased Confidence: CD provides confidence that your application can be deployed to production at any time.
- Faster Feedback: You can get faster feedback from users on new features and updates, allowing you to iterate and improve your application more quickly.

Implementing CD for Go Applications

Here's a general outline of how you can implement CD for your Go applications:

1. Choose a CD Tool: Select a CD tool that meets your needs and integrates with your chosen cloud platform and infrastructure. Popular options include Argo CD, Spinnaker, and cloud provider CD services (e.g., AWS CodePipeline, Azure DevOps).
2. Define Your Deployment Pipeline: Define the stages of your deployment pipeline, including build, test, deploy to staging, run acceptance tests, and deploy to production. You might also include manual approval steps or other custom actions.
3. Automate Deployments: Automate the deployment process to your target environments (staging and production). This might involve using tools like kubectl for Kubernetes deployments, scripting deployments to virtual machines, or using serverless deployment platforms.

4. Set Up Monitoring and Rollback: Configure monitoring and alerting to track the health and performance of your deployed application. Implement a rollback strategy to quickly revert to a previous version if any issues are detected.

Example: Deploying to Kubernetes with Argo CD

Argo CD is a popular continuous delivery tool for Kubernetes that follows the GitOps approach. You define your desired application state in Git, and Argo CD automatically synchronizes your Kubernetes cluster with that state.

To deploy a Go application with Argo CD:

1. Package your application as a Docker image.
2. Define your Kubernetes deployment and service configurations in YAML files.
3. Store these files in a Git repository.
4. Configure Argo CD to monitor your repository and deploy the application to your Kubernetes cluster.

Real-World Examples

Many companies use CD to streamline their release processes:

-   Amazon: Amazon uses CD to deploy updates to its e-commerce platform multiple times a day.
-   Netflix: Netflix uses CD to deploy new features and bug fixes to its streaming service quickly and reliably.
-   Etsy: Etsy uses CD to deploy changes to its website and backend systems, allowing them to experiment with new features and respond to user feedback rapidly.

By implementing CD for your Go applications, you can achieve a more efficient and reliable release process, enabling you to deliver value to your users faster and with greater confidence.

Chapter 11: Performance Optimization

You've built a solid Go application, it's functioning correctly, and it's secure. But what if it's slow? What if it consumes too much memory or struggles to handle a large number of requests? That's where performance optimization comes in. Think of it like tuning a race car. You might have a powerful engine, but to achieve peak performance, you need to fine-tune the engine, optimize the aerodynamics, and reduce unnecessary weight. Similarly, performance optimization in Go involves analyzing your code, identifying bottlenecks, and applying techniques to make it faster, more efficient, and more scalable.

In this chapter, we'll explore how to profile Go code, optimize for memory and CPU usage, apply performance tuning techniques, and conduct benchmarking and performance testing.

11.1 Profiling Go Code

Profiling is a crucial technique for understanding and improving the performance of your Go applications. Profiling is like using an X-ray to look inside your code and see how it's behaving, revealing which parts are consuming the most resources and where potential bottlenecks might be hiding. Think of it like this: you have a car that's not running as smoothly as it should. You could guess what's wrong, but it's more effective to use diagnostic tools to pinpoint the exact issue. Profiling provides those diagnostic tools for your Go code, allowing you to identify performance bottlenecks and optimize your application for speed and efficiency.

Profiling is the process of collecting and analyzing data about your program's execution. This data can include:

- CPU usage: Which functions are consuming the most CPU time?

- Memory allocation: Where is memory being allocated, and are there any memory leaks?
- Blocking operations: Which parts of your code are spending the most time waiting for operations like network requests or disk I/O?
- Goroutine behavior: How many goroutines are running, and are there any deadlocks or race conditions?

By analyzing this profiling data, you can gain insights into your application's performance characteristics and identify areas for optimization.

Go's Built-in Profiling Tools

Go provides excellent built-in tools for profiling your code:

- pprof package: The pprof package in the standard library is your gateway to profiling in Go. It provides functions for collecting and analyzing various types of profiling data.
- Profiling flags: You can enable profiling by passing specific flags to the go test command. For example:
  - go test -cpuprofile=cpu.prof: Generates a CPU profile, showing which functions are using the most CPU time.
  - go test -memprofile=mem.prof: Generates a memory profile, revealing memory allocation patterns and potential leaks.
  - go test -blockprofile=block.prof: Generates a block profile, showing where goroutines are blocked waiting for resources.
  - go test -trace=trace.out: Generates a trace file, capturing events and timing information about goroutine execution.
- pprof tool: The pprof tool is a command-line tool that allows you to analyze the profiling data generated by your Go programs. It provides various commands and

visualizations to help you understand the data and identify performance bottlenecks.

Example: Generating and Analyzing a CPU Profile

Let's walk through an example of how to generate and analyze a CPU profile for your Go code:

1. **Write a Benchmark:** First, you need a benchmark function to profile. Benchmarks are functions that measure the performance of a specific piece of code.

```Go
package mypackage

import "testing"

func fibonacci(n int) int {

    if n <= 1 {

        return n

    }

    return fibonacci(n-1) + fibonacci(n-2)

}

func BenchmarkFibonacci(b *testing.B) {

    for i := 0; i < b.N; i++ {

        fibonacci(30) // Benchmark the fibonacci
function with input 30

    }
```

}

2. **Generate the Profile:** Run the benchmark with the -cpuprofile flag to generate a CPU profile:

```Bash
go test -bench=. -cpuprofile=cpu.prof
```

This command runs all benchmarks in the current directory (specified by -bench=.) and generates a CPU profile named cpu.prof.

3. **Analyze the Profile:** Use the pprof tool to analyze the profile:

```Bash
go tool pprof cpu.prof
```

This opens an interactive console where you can explore the profiling data. You can use commands like top to see the functions that consume the most CPU time, list to view the source code of specific functions, and web to generate an interactive call graph in your web browser.

Interpreting the Profiling Data

The pprof tool provides various ways to visualize and analyze the profiling data. You can look for:

- Functions with high CPU usage: Identify functions that consume a significant portion of the CPU time. These might be good candidates for optimization.

- Call graphs: Visualize the call relationships between functions to understand how execution flows through your code.
- Memory allocation patterns: Identify areas where memory is being allocated excessively or where potential memory leaks might exist.

Real-World Examples

Profiling is used extensively in real-world Go projects to optimize performance:

- Docker: The Docker team uses profiling to identify and optimize performance bottlenecks in the Docker engine.
- Kubernetes: The Kubernetes project uses profiling to improve the efficiency and scalability of the Kubernetes control plane.
- High-Performance Applications: Developers of high-performance applications, such as databases and game servers, rely heavily on profiling to achieve optimal performance.

11.2 Optimizing for Memory and CPU Usage

Once you've identified performance bottlenecks in your Go code through profiling, it's time to roll up your sleeves and start optimizing. This involves making changes to your code to reduce resource consumption, improve efficiency, and ultimately make your application faster and more scalable. Think of it like tuning a musical instrument. You might have a beautiful instrument, but to achieve the best sound, you need to adjust the strings, tune the keys, and ensure all the parts are working in harmony. Similarly, optimizing your Go code involves fine-tuning its different aspects to achieve optimal performance.

Let's explore how to optimize your Go code for both memory and CPU usage.

Optimizing Memory Usage

Memory is a precious resource in any application, and Go is no exception. Optimizing memory usage can lead to significant performance improvements, especially when dealing with large datasets or high-traffic applications.

Here are some key strategies for optimizing memory usage in your Go programs:

- Reduce Allocations: Every time you create a new object or data structure in Go, memory is allocated for it. Reducing the number of unnecessary allocations can significantly improve memory efficiency. Consider these techniques:
    - Object Pooling: Reuse objects instead of creating new ones every time. Create a pool of objects that can be reused, reducing the overhead of memory allocation.
    - Buffers: Use buffers to pre-allocate memory for operations that involve reading or writing data. This avoids repeated allocations as the data grows.
    - Avoid Temporary Objects: Minimize the creation of temporary objects that are only used briefly. Sometimes, you can refactor your code to avoid creating these temporary objects altogether.
- Efficient Data Structures: Choosing the right data structure for your task can have a significant impact on memory usage.
    - Maps: Use maps when you need fast lookups by key.
    - Slices: Use slices when you need ordered collections or when you need to append or remove elements efficiently.

- Structs: Use structs to represent complex data structures. Consider packing struct fields to reduce memory usage.
- Avoid Memory Leaks: A memory leak occurs when memory is allocated but never released, even when it's no longer needed. This can eventually lead to your application running out of memory.
  - Close Resources: Ensure that you close resources like file handles, network connections, and channels when you're done with them.
  - Defer Statements: Use defer statements to ensure that resources are closed even if errors occur.

Example: Reducing Allocations with a Buffer

```go
Go

// Inefficient code (repeated allocations)

var data []byte

for {

    // ... read data into a small buffer ...

    data = append(data, buffer...)

}

// Efficient code (using a pre-allocated buffer)

buffer := make([]byte, 1024) // Pre-allocate a
buffer

data := make([]byte, 0, 1024) // Create a slice
with initial capacity

for {
```

```
// ... read data into the buffer ...

    data = append(data, buffer[:n]...) // Append
only the necessary data

}
```

In the efficient code, we pre-allocate a buffer and reuse it for each read operation, reducing the number of memory allocations.

Optimizing CPU Usage

Optimizing CPU usage is about making your code run faster and more efficiently. This involves reducing unnecessary computations, choosing efficient algorithms, and utilizing concurrency effectively.

Here are some strategies for optimizing CPU usage in your Go programs:

- Optimize Algorithms and Data Structures: Choosing the right algorithm and data structure for your task can significantly impact performance. Consider the time complexity of different algorithms and choose the most efficient one for your needs.
- Avoid Unnecessary Computations: Eliminate redundant calculations or unnecessary loops. Sometimes, you can refactor your code to avoid performing the same computations multiple times.
- Concurrency: Go's concurrency features (goroutines and channels) allow you to parallelize tasks and utilize multiple CPU cores. Use goroutines to perform independent tasks concurrently and channels to communicate between them.
- Avoid Blocking Operations: Blocking operations, like network requests or disk I/O, can stall your program's execution. Use asynchronous techniques or non-blocking

I/O to allow your program to continue executing while waiting for these operations to complete.

Example: Using Goroutines for Concurrency

```go
Go

// Sequential processing

for _, item := range items {

    processItem(item)

}

// Concurrent processing with goroutines

var wg sync.WaitGroup

wg.Add(len(items))

for _, item := range items {

    go func(item Item) {

        defer wg.Done()

        processItem(item)

    }(item)

}

wg.Wait()
```

In the concurrent code, we use goroutines to process each item concurrently, potentially utilizing multiple CPU cores and speeding up the processing.

Real-World Examples

Optimizing for memory and CPU usage is crucial in many real-world applications:

- High-Performance Computing: Applications like scientific simulations and financial modeling require efficient use of CPU and memory to handle complex computations.
- Web Servers: Web servers need to handle a large number of concurrent requests efficiently, requiring optimized memory and CPU usage to maintain performance and responsiveness.
- Data Processing Pipelines: Data processing pipelines often deal with large datasets, requiring efficient memory management and CPU utilization to process data quickly.

By applying these optimization techniques and carefully considering memory and CPU usage, you can build Go applications that are fast, efficient, and scalable.

11.3 Performance Tuning Techniques

Let's discuss some specific performance tuning techniques that can help you squeeze even more speed and efficiency out of your Go applications. These techniques are like fine-tuning the gears and adjusting the carburetor of your car to get that extra boost of performance.

1. Connection Pooling

When your Go application interacts with a database, establishing a new connection for each query can be an expensive operation. It involves network communication, authentication, and resource allocation. Connection pooling helps optimize this process by maintaining a pool of open connections that can be reused for multiple queries.

Think of it like a taxi service. Instead of calling a new taxi every time you need a ride, you have a pool of taxis waiting, ready to pick up passengers. This reduces the waiting time and makes the transportation system more efficient.

In Go, you can use the database/sql package with a connection pool to manage database connections efficiently.

Example: Using Connection Pooling with database/sql

```Go
package main

import (

    "database/sql"

    "fmt"

    "log"

    "time"

    _ "github.com/go-sql-driver/mysql"

)

func main() {

    // ... (Database connection details) ...

    db, err := sql.Open("mysql",
dbConnectionString)

    if err != nil {

        log.Fatal(err)

    }
```

```
    defer db.Close()

    // Configure connection pool

    db.SetMaxIdleConns(10)   // Maximum number of
idle connections in the pool

    db.SetMaxOpenConns(100) // Maximum number of
open connections to the database

    db.SetConnMaxLifetime(time.Hour) // Maximum
lifetime of a connection

    // ... (Use the db object to execute
queries) ...

}
```

In this example:

- db.SetMaxIdleConns(10) sets the maximum number of idle connections that can remain open in the pool.
- db.SetMaxOpenConns(100) sets the maximum number of open connections to the database.
- db.SetConnMaxLifetime(time.Hour) sets the maximum lifetime of a connection in the pool. After this duration, the connection will be closed and replaced with a new one.

2. Caching

Caching is a powerful technique for improving performance by storing frequently accessed data in a cache, which is a temporary storage area that is faster to access than the original data source.

Think of it like keeping frequently used items within easy reach. Instead of going to the basement every time you need a tool, you keep the most commonly used ones in your toolbox.

Various caching strategies can be used in your Go applications:

- In-Memory Caching: Store cached data in memory using tools like sync.Map or third-party libraries like go-cache or bigcache.
- Distributed Caching: Use a distributed cache like Redis or Memcached to store cached data across multiple servers, improving scalability and availability.
- CDN Caching: Use a Content Delivery Network (CDN) to cache static assets (like images, CSS, and JavaScript) closer to your users, reducing latency and improving page load times.

Example: In-Memory Caching with sync.Map

```go
Go

package main

import (

    "fmt"

    "sync"

)

var cache sync.Map // In-memory cache

func getCachedData(key string) (interface{},
bool) {

    return cache.Load(key)

}

func setCachedData(key string, value interface{})
{

    cache.Store(key, value)
```

```go
}

func main() {

    // ... (Your application logic) ...

    // Get data from the cache

    if data, ok := getCachedData("my_key"); ok {

        fmt.Println("Data from cache:", data)

    } else {

        // Data not in cache, fetch it from the
source

        data = fetchDataFromSource()

        setCachedData("my_key", data)

        fmt.Println("Data from source:", data)

    }

    // ... (Use the data) ...

}
```

In this example, we use sync.Map to store cached data in memory. The getCachedData function checks if the data is in the cache, and if not, it fetches it from the source and stores it in the cache.

3. Code Optimization Techniques

- Use Efficient Algorithms and Data Structures: Choose algorithms and data structures that are efficient for your use case. Consider the time and space complexity of different options.

- Avoid Unnecessary Operations: Eliminate redundant calculations, unnecessary loops, or repeated function calls.
- Optimize String Concatenation: Use strings.Builder or bytes.Buffer for efficient string concatenation, especially when concatenating many strings.
- Preallocate Slices: When you know the approximate size of a slice, preallocate it to avoid unnecessary reallocations as it grows.

4. Compiler Optimizations

Go provides compiler optimizations that can improve the performance of your code. You can enable these optimizations by passing flags to the go build command.

- Inlining: The compiler can inline small functions, eliminating the overhead of function calls.
- Escape Analysis: The compiler can determine if variables escape to the heap or can be allocated on the stack, which is more efficient.
- Dead Code Elimination: The compiler can remove unreachable or unused code.

Example: Enabling Compiler Optimizations

Bash

```
go build -gcflags="-m"
```

The -gcflags="-m" flag enables more aggressive compiler optimizations.

5. Asynchronous Operations

Use asynchronous operations (goroutines and channels) to avoid blocking the main thread of your application while waiting for long-running tasks like network requests or disk I/O.

6. Profiling and Monitoring in Production

Continuously profile and monitor your application in production to identify and address performance issues. Use tools like Prometheus, Grafana, and Jaeger to collect and visualize metrics, traces, and logs.

Real-World Examples

These performance tuning techniques are used in various real-world applications:

- High-Traffic Websites: Websites like Google, Facebook, and Amazon use caching extensively to handle millions of requests per second.
- Databases: Databases use connection pooling and caching to optimize query performance.
- Game Servers: Game servers use asynchronous operations and code optimizations to handle real-time interactions with many players.

11.4 Benchmarking and Performance Testing

Benchmarking and performance testing techniques are like using a stopwatch and a measuring tape to quantify the speed and efficiency of your application. They help you understand how your code performs under different conditions and identify areas for improvement.

Think of it like this: you've built a new bicycle, and you want to know how fast it can go. You could just ride it around the block and get a general sense of its speed, but to get a precise measurement, you would use a stopwatch and a measured track. Benchmarking and performance testing provide those precise measurements for your Go code.

Benchmarking

Benchmarking involves running a specific piece of code multiple times and measuring its execution time, memory allocations, and other performance metrics. Go provides a built-in benchmarking framework with the testing package, making it easy to write and run benchmarks.

Writing Benchmarks in Go

Benchmark functions in Go have a specific signature:

Go

```go
func BenchmarkMyFunction(b *testing.B) {

    // Benchmarking code here

}
```

The b *testing.B parameter provides methods for controlling the benchmark execution, such as b.N, which represents the number of iterations to run.

Inside the benchmark function, you typically place the code you want to benchmark within a loop that runs b.N times. This ensures that the benchmark runs long enough to provide meaningful measurements.

Example: Benchmarking String Concatenation

Go

```go
package mypackage

import (

    "strings"
```

```
    "testing"

)

func BenchmarkStringConcatenationPlus(b
*testing.B) {

    for i := 0; i < b.N; i++ {

        _ = "hello" + " " + "world"

    }

}

func BenchmarkStringConcatenationBuilder(b
*testing.B) {

    for i := 0; i < b.N; i++ {

        var sb strings.Builder

        sb.WriteString("hello")

        sb.WriteString(" ")

        sb.WriteString("world")

        _ = sb.String()

    }

}
```

This code defines two benchmarks:

- BenchmarkStringConcatenationPlus: Measures the performance of string concatenation using the + operator.

- **BenchmarkStringConcatenationBuilder**: Measures the performance of string concatenation using stringBuilder essential.

Running Benchmarks

You can run benchmarks using the go test command with the -bench flag:

Bash

```
go test -bench=.
```

This command runs all benchmarks in the current directory. The output will show the execution time per operation for each benchmark, allowing you to compare the performance of different approaches.

Performance Testing

While benchmarking focuses on measuring the performance of isolated code snippets, performance testing takes a broader approach. It involves simulating real-world scenarios and measuring the performance of your entire application under different load conditions.

This helps you understand how your application behaves when multiple users access it concurrently, identify performance bottlenecks, and ensure that it can handle the expected traffic.

Steps in Performance Testing:

1. Define Performance Goals: Determine your application's performance goals, such as response times, throughput, and resource utilization.
2. Create Test Scenarios: Create realistic test scenarios that simulate user behavior and traffic patterns.

3. Choose Load Testing Tools: Select load testing tools that can generate the desired traffic and collect performance metrics.
4. Run the Tests: Execute the performance tests and collect data on response times, throughput, error rates, and resource utilization.
5. Analyze the Results: Analyze the test results to identify performance bottlenecks and areas for improvement.

Tools for Performance Testing

Several tools can help you conduct performance testing:

- k6: An open-source load testing tool that allows you to write performance tests in JavaScript.
- JMeter: A popular open-source load testing tool with a graphical user interface.
- Locust: A scalable load testing tool written in Python.
- Cloud Provider Load Testing Services: AWS, Azure, and GCP offer their own load testing services.

Real-World Examples

Benchmarking and performance testing are essential for building high-performance applications:

- Web Applications: Performance testing helps ensure that web applications can handle peak traffic loads and provide a good user experience.
- Databases: Benchmarking is used to compare the performance of different database queries and optimize database performance.
- Game Servers: Performance testing helps ensure that game servers can handle a large number of concurrent players without lag or performance issues.

By incorporating benchmarking and performance testing into your development process, you can gain valuable insights into the performance of your Go applications, identify areas for optimization, and ensure that your applications are fast, efficient, and scalable

Chapter 12: Building a Real-World Cloud-Native Application

You've learned about Go, databases, microservices, security, testing, and even how to deploy your applications to the cloud. Now, let's put all those pieces together and build a real-world cloud-native application with Go. This is where you get to see how all those concepts come together in a practical project. In this chapter, we'll walk through the process of building a simple e-commerce application with a microservices architecture, using Go for the backend and deploying it to the cloud with Docker and Kubernetes.

12.1 Project Overview and Requirements

Let's build a real-world cloud-native application with Go. We'll create a simplified e-commerce platform, putting into practice the concepts and techniques we've explored throughout this book. Think of it like a capstone project where you get to apply your newfound Go skills to build something tangible and practical.

Our e-commerce application, which we'll call "GoShop," will provide a platform for users to browse products, add them to their shopping carts, and place orders. It will demonstrate how to build a backend system with a microservices architecture, using Go for the backend and deploying it to the cloud with Docker and Kubernetes.

Core Features

GoShop will have the following core features:

- **Product Catalog:**
  - Users can browse a catalog of products.
  - Each product will have details like name, description, price, and image.

- Users can search and filter products based on various criteria (e.g., category, price range).
- **Shopping Cart:**
  - Users can add products to their shopping cart.
  - They can view the contents of their cart, including the total price.
  - They can remove items from their cart.
- **Order Placement:**
  - Users can proceed to checkout and place orders.
  - They can provide shipping and payment information.
  - The system will generate an order confirmation.
- **Order History:**
  - Users can view their past orders, including their status (e.g., pending, shipped, delivered).
  - They can view the details of each order, including the items purchased and the total price.
- **User Accounts:**
  - Users can create accounts with a username and password.
  - They can log in to their accounts to access their shopping cart and order history.

Microservices Architecture

To build a scalable and maintainable system, we'll use a microservices architecture. This means breaking down the application into smaller, independent services, each responsible for a specific business capability.

GoShop will have the following microservices:

- Product Catalog Service: Manages the product catalog, including adding, updating, deleting, and retrieving product information.

- Shopping Cart Service: Manages user shopping carts, allowing users to add and remove items and calculate the total price.
- Order Service: Handles order placement, processing payments, and updating order status.
- User Service: Manages user accounts, including registration, login, and authentication.

Technology Stack

- Programming Language: Go
- Database: PostgreSQL
- Message Queue: RabbitMQ
- Cache: Redis
- Containerization: Docker
- Orchestration: Kubernetes
- API Gateway: (To be chosen based on your preference - Kong, Tyk, etc.)

Communication

- REST: We'll use RESTful APIs for communication between the API gateway and the microservices. This allows for easy integration with various clients and front-end applications.
- gRPC: We'll use gRPC for internal communication between microservices. This provides a more efficient and performant way for services to interact within the system.

Deployment

We'll deploy GoShop to a cloud platform (AWS, Azure, or GCP) using Docker and Kubernetes. This will allow us to:

- Containerize each microservice: Package each service and its dependencies into a Docker container for portability and consistency.
- Orchestrate the containers: Use Kubernetes to manage the deployment, scaling, and networking of the containers.

- Scale the application: Easily scale the application by adding or removing instances of each microservice as needed.

Non-Functional Requirements

In addition to the core features, we'll also consider some non-functional requirements:

- Performance: The application should be performant and responsive, even under high load.
- Scalability: The application should be able to scale to handle increasing traffic and data.
- Reliability: The application should be reliable and fault-tolerant, minimizing downtime.
- Security: The application should be secure, protecting user data and preventing unauthorized access.
- Maintainability: The codebase should be well-organized and easy to maintain.

By clearly defining the project overview and requirements, we establish a solid foundation for building our GoShop application. In the following sections, we'll delve into the design, implementation, and deployment of this real-world cloud-native application.

12.2 Designing the Application Architecture

Now that we have a clear understanding of the goals and requirements for our GoShop e-commerce application, let's design the architecture that will bring it to life. This architecture will serve as the blueprint for our system, guiding how we organize the different components, how they interact, and how we deploy and scale the application.

Think of it like designing the floor plan for a house. You need to consider the different rooms (services), their purposes, how they connect, and how people (requests) will flow through the house. A well-designed architecture ensures that the house is functional, efficient, and comfortable to live in.

Key Components

Our GoShop architecture will consist of the following key components:

- API Gateway: The API gateway acts as the single entry point for all incoming requests to the application. It handles authentication, authorization, routing, and other cross-cutting concerns. Think of it like the front door of our house, directing visitors to the appropriate rooms.
- Microservices: We'll break down the application's functionality into separate microservices, each responsible for a specific business capability. These microservices will communicate with each other to fulfill user requests. In our house analogy, these are the individual rooms – the kitchen, the living room, the bedrooms – each serving a distinct purpose.
- Database: A database will store the application's data, such as product information, user accounts, and orders. This is like the storage room in our house, where we keep our belongings organized and accessible.
- Message Queue: A message queue will facilitate asynchronous communication between microservices. This allows services to send messages to each other without waiting for an immediate response, improving scalability and decoupling. Think of it like a mailbox where services can leave messages for each other.
- Cache: A cache will store frequently accessed data to improve performance and reduce the load on the database. This is like keeping frequently used items within easy reach, so you don't have to go searching for them every time.

Communication

- REST: We'll use RESTful APIs for communication between the API gateway and the microservices. This provides a standardized and widely understood way for different parts of the system to interact. It's like having clear signs and directions within our house, so visitors can easily find their way around.
- gRPC: We'll use gRPC for internal communication between microservices. gRPC offers better performance and efficiency compared to REST, making it suitable for communication within the system where latency and bandwidth are important considerations. It's like having efficient internal pathways within our house for quick and easy movement between rooms.

Deployment

- Docker: We'll containerize each microservice using Docker. This packages each service and its dependencies into a portable unit that can be easily deployed and run on any system with Docker installed. It's like packing each room of our house into a separate, self-contained module that can be easily transported and assembled.
- Kubernetes: We'll deploy and orchestrate the containers using Kubernetes. Kubernetes provides a platform for managing and scaling containerized applications, automating tasks like deployment, networking, and health checks. It's like having a smart home system that manages the different modules (rooms) of our house, ensuring they are functioning correctly and efficiently.

Architecture Diagram

Here's a simplified diagram that illustrates the GoShop architecture:

```
[API Gateway] --> [Product Catalog Service]

                  [Shopping Cart Service]

                  [Order Service]

                  [User Service]

[Microservices] <--> [Database]

[Microservices] <--> [Message Queue]

[Microservices] <--> [Cache]
```

Real-World Examples

This architecture is similar to how many modern e-commerce platforms are built:

- Amazon: Amazon uses a microservices architecture to break down its massive e-commerce platform into smaller, manageable services.
- Netflix: Netflix uses a microservices architecture to power its streaming service, handling millions of users and videos.
- Uber: Uber uses a microservices architecture to manage its ride-hailing platform, connecting riders and drivers efficiently.

Benefits of This Architecture

- Scalability: The microservices architecture allows us to scale each service independently based on its needs.
- Resilience: If one service fails, the other services can continue to function.
- Maintainability: Smaller, independent services are easier to understand, maintain, and update.
- Flexibility: We can use different technologies and programming languages for different services if needed.

Carefully designing the architecture of our GoShop application, we lay the foundation for a scalable, resilient, and maintainable system. In the following sections, we'll implement the microservices, set up the infrastructure, and deploy the application to the cloud.

12.3 Implementing Microservices with Go

Now that we have a solid architectural plan for our GoShop application, it's time to roll up our sleeves and start building the microservices that will power it. This is where we'll put our Go knowledge to work, crafting the backend logic that handles user requests, manages data, and orchestrates the interactions between different parts of the system.

Think of it like constructing the individual rooms of our house. We have the floor plan, and now we need to build the walls, install the plumbing and electrical systems, and furnish each room according to its purpose.

Go: The Language of Choice

We'll use Go as our programming language for implementing the microservices. Go is well-suited for this task due to its:

- Efficiency: Go's compiled nature and efficient runtime make it ideal for building lightweight and performant services.
- Concurrency: Go's built-in concurrency features (goroutines and channels) make it easy to handle concurrent requests and build responsive services.
- Strong Ecosystem: Go has a rich ecosystem of libraries and frameworks for building web servers, APIs, and interacting with databases.
- Cloud-Native Support: Go is designed with modern cloud environments in mind, making it easy to containerize and deploy microservices on platforms like Docker and Kubernetes.

Microservice Implementation

Let's start by implementing the Product Catalog Service. This service will be responsible for managing product information, including:

- Adding new products: Allowing administrators to add new products to the catalog.
- Updating product details: Enabling updates to product information like name, description, price, and image.
- Deleting products: Removing products from the catalog.
- Retrieving product information: Providing an API for other services (and potentially the frontend) to fetch product details.

Here's a basic outline of the Go code for the Product Catalog Service:

```go
Go

package main

import (

    "context"

    "encoding/json"

    "fmt"

    "log"

    "net/http"

    "github.com/gorilla/mux"

    "google.golang.org/grpc"

    "gorm.io/driver/postgres"
```

```go
    "gorm.io/gorm"

)

// Product struct representing the product data
model

type Product struct {

    gorm.Model

    Name        string  `json:"name"`

    Description string  `json:"description"`

    Price       float64 `json:"price"`

    ImageURL    string  `json:"image_url"`

}

// Database connection and GORM setup

var db *gorm.DB

func init() {

    dsn := "host=localhost user=postgres
password=password dbname=goshop port=5432
TimeZone=Asia/Shanghai"

    var err error

    db, err = gorm.Open(postgres.Open(dsn),
&gorm.Config{})

    if err != nil {

        panic("failed to connect database")
```

```go
    }

    // AutoMigrate the schema

    db.AutoMigrate(&Product{})

}

// HTTP handler functions for REST API endpoints

func getProductsHandler(w http.ResponseWriter, r
*http.Request) {

    var products []Product

    db.Find(&products)

    json.NewEncoder(w).Encode(products)

}

func getProductHandler(w http.ResponseWriter, r
*http.Request) {

    vars := mux.Vars(r)

    id := vars["id"]

    var product Product

    db.First(&product, id)

    json.NewEncoder(w).Encode(product)

}

// ... (Other handler functions for adding,
updating, deleting products) ...

func main() {
```

```go
    router := mux.NewRouter()

    router.HandleFunc("/products",
getProductsHandler).Methods("GET")

    router.HandleFunc("/products/{id}",
getProductHandler).Methods("GET")

    // ... (Other routes for adding, updating,
deleting products) ...

    // ... (gRPC server setup for internal
communication) ...

    log.Fatal(http.ListenAndServe(":8080",
router))

}
```

In this code:

- We define a Product struct to represent the product data model.
- We set up a connection to the PostgreSQL database using GORM.
- We define HTTP handler functions for REST API endpoints to retrieve products (getProductsHandler, getProductHandler) and potentially other actions like adding, updating, and deleting products.
- We set up a gRPC server for internal communication with other services (not shown in this simplified example).

Implementing Other Microservices

You would follow a similar approach to implement the other microservices:

- **Shopping Cart Service:**

- Implement endpoints to add and remove items from the cart.
- Calculate the total price of the cart.
- Store cart data in Redis for persistence and quick retrieval.
- **Order Service:**
  - Implement endpoints to create and manage orders.
  - Process payments using a payment gateway integration.
  - Update order status (e.g., pending, shipped, delivered).
  - Communicate with other services (like Product Catalog Service and User Service) using gRPC to retrieve product and user information.
- **User Service:**
  - Implement endpoints for user registration and login.
  - Handle authentication and authorization.
  - Store user data securely in the database.

Real-World Considerations

- Error Handling: Implement robust error handling in each microservice to gracefully handle errors and provide informative responses.
- Logging: Use structured logging to record events and errors for debugging and monitoring.
- Testing: Write comprehensive tests (unit, integration, and potentially E2E) for each microservice to ensure its functionality and reliability.

By implementing these microservices with Go, you create the building blocks for your e-commerce application. Each service focuses on a specific task, communicates with others through well-defined APIs, and contributes to the overall functionality of the system.

12.4 Deploying and Scaling the Application

You've built the microservices that power your GoShop application, and now it's time to deploy them to the cloud and make them accessible to the world. This involves packaging your services, choosing a cloud provider, and leveraging tools like Docker and Kubernetes to orchestrate and scale your application.

Think of it like launching a fleet of ships. You've built the individual ships (microservices), and now you need to choose a harbor (cloud provider), equip them with navigation systems (Docker), and coordinate their movements (Kubernetes) to ensure they reach their destinations safely and efficiently.

1. Containerization with Docker

First, we need to package each microservice into a Docker container. This creates a portable and self-contained unit that includes the service's code, dependencies, and runtime environment.

- Create Dockerfiles: For each microservice, you'll create a Dockerfile that specifies the base image, copies the application code and dependencies, and defines the commands to run the service.
- Build Docker Images: Use the docker build command to build Docker images for each microservice.
- Push Images to a Registry: Push the Docker images to a container registry (like Docker Hub, Amazon ECR, or Google Container Registry) so that they can be easily accessed during deployment.

2. Choose a Cloud Provider and Kubernetes Cluster

Next, you'll choose a cloud provider (AWS, Azure, or GCP) that meets your needs and create a Kubernetes cluster on that provider.

Kubernetes will manage the deployment, scaling, and networking of your containers.

- Managed Kubernetes Services: Consider using managed Kubernetes services like Amazon EKS, Azure AKS, or Google GKE to simplify cluster management.

3. Deploy to Kubernetes

Once you have a Kubernetes cluster, you'll deploy your GoShop microservices to it. This involves creating Kubernetes configuration files (YAML files) that define your deployments, services, and other resources.

- Deployments: Create deployments for each microservice, specifying the Docker image to use, the number of replicas (instances), and any environment variables or configurations.
- Services: Create services to expose your microservices internally and externally. Services provide a stable endpoint for accessing your applications, even if the underlying pods change.
- Ingresses: If you need to expose your services to the internet, create ingresses to route external traffic to the appropriate services.

4. API Gateway Integration

Configure your API gateway to route incoming requests to the appropriate microservices. The API gateway can handle tasks like authentication, authorization, rate limiting, and request transformation.

5. Database and Message Queue Setup

Provision and configure your database (e.g., PostgreSQL) and message queue (e.g., RabbitMQ) on your cloud provider. These services will be used by your microservices to store data and communicate with each other.

6. Caching

Set up a caching layer (e.g., Redis) to store frequently accessed data and improve application performance.

7. Monitoring and Logging

Implement monitoring and logging to track the health and performance of your application. Use tools like Prometheus, Grafana, and Jaeger to collect and visualize metrics, traces, and logs.

Scaling Your Application

Kubernetes provides several mechanisms for scaling your application:

- Horizontal Pod Autoscaler (HPA): HPA automatically adjusts the number of pods (replicas) for a deployment based on CPU or memory usage. This allows your application to scale dynamically based on demand.
- Manual Scaling: You can manually scale your deployments by changing the number of replicas in the deployment configuration.
- Cluster Autoscaler: Cluster autoscaler automatically adjusts the size of your Kubernetes cluster by adding or removing nodes based on the resource requirements of your deployments.

Real-World Examples

Many companies use similar approaches to deploy and scale their applications:

- Spotify: Uses Kubernetes to deploy and scale its music streaming platform, handling millions of users and songs.
- Airbnb: Uses Kubernetes to manage its services, including search, payments, and user management, ensuring high availability and scalability.
- Pinterest: Uses Kubernetes to deploy and scale its image-sharing platform, serving billions of pins and recommendations.

By following these steps and leveraging the power of Docker and Kubernetes, you can deploy and scale your GoShop application in the cloud, ensuring that it can handle real-world traffic and provide a reliable and performant experience for your users.

Chapter 13: Analyzing Production-Ready Codebases

In this chapter, we'll explore open-source Go projects, discuss architectural patterns and best practices, and see how you can learn from real-world examples to improve your own Go backend development skills.

13.1 Open-Source Go Projects for Backend Development

One of the best ways to accelerate your growth as a Go developer and gain insights into building production-ready backend systems is to study real-world codebases. The Go ecosystem is teeming with open-source projects that showcase best practices, architectural patterns, and clever solutions to common challenges. It's like having a backstage pass to observe how experienced developers tackle real-world problems, allowing you to learn from their techniques and apply them to your own projects.

Think of it like this: you're an aspiring chef, and you want to learn how to create gourmet dishes. You could read cookbooks and watch cooking shows, but there's nothing quite like observing a master chef in action, seeing how they combine ingredients, apply techniques, and create culinary masterpieces. Similarly, studying open-source Go projects gives you a firsthand look at how skilled developers build high-quality backend systems.

In this section, we'll explore some notable open-source Go projects that are particularly relevant for backend development. We'll examine their code structure, design choices, and how they address common backend challenges.

1. Docker

Docker, the widely used containerization platform, is largely written in Go. Its codebase is a goldmine of knowledge for backend developers, demonstrating how to:

- Handle concurrency: Docker extensively uses goroutines and channels to manage containers, handle network requests, and orchestrate complex operations concurrently. Studying its code can teach you how to write efficient and concurrent Go programs that can handle many tasks simultaneously.
- Build command-line interfaces (CLIs): The docker CLI is a powerful tool for interacting with the Docker daemon. By examining its code, you can learn how to build user-friendly and robust CLIs in Go, handling user input, options, and output effectively.
- Work with system APIs: Docker interacts with the operating system's kernel to manage containers and resources. Its code demonstrates how to use Go to interact with system-level APIs, providing insights into low-level programming and system interactions.
- Implement logging and error handling: Docker's codebase showcases robust logging and error handling practices, which are essential for building reliable and maintainable systems. You can learn how to effectively log events, handle errors gracefully, and provide informative error messages.

2. Kubernetes

Kubernetes, the leading container orchestration system, is also primarily written in Go. Its codebase is a vast and complex system that offers many learning opportunities for backend developers:

- Microservices architecture: Kubernetes itself is built as a collection of microservices, providing a real-world example of how to design and implement a distributed system. You can learn how to decompose a complex application into smaller, manageable services that communicate with each other.

- API design: Kubernetes exposes a comprehensive API for managing clusters and applications. Studying its API design can teach you how to build well-structured and RESTful APIs in Go, handling different HTTP methods, request parameters, and response formats.
- Networking: Kubernetes manages complex networking between containers and services. Its code demonstrates how to handle networking challenges in a distributed environment, including service discovery, load balancing, and network policies.
- Resource management: Kubernetes manages resources like CPU, memory, and storage, showcasing how to handle resource allocation and scheduling in a Go application. You can learn how to efficiently allocate resources to containers and ensure that your application runs smoothly.

3. etcd

etcd is a distributed key-value store that is often used for service discovery and configuration management in distributed systems. Its codebase is a great example of:

- Distributed systems concepts: etcd is a distributed system that uses the Raft consensus algorithm to ensure data consistency across multiple nodes. Studying its code can teach you about distributed consensus, fault tolerance, and how to build reliable distributed systems in Go.
- Concurrency and synchronization: etcd handles concurrent requests and ensures data consistency using goroutines, channels, and synchronization primitives like mutexes and condition variables. You can learn how to write concurrent Go code that is safe and efficient.
- Networking and communication: etcd uses gRPC for efficient communication between nodes. You can learn how

to use gRPC in a real-world application and understand its benefits for inter-service communication.

4. Traefik

Traefik is a modern reverse proxy and load balancer that is designed for microservices and cloud-native environments. Its codebase demonstrates:

- Networking and proxying: Traefik handles incoming network requests and routes them to the appropriate backend services. You can learn how to build reverse proxies in Go and handle HTTP requests and responses effectively.
- Dynamic configuration: Traefik can dynamically configure itself based on service discovery mechanisms and automatically update its routing rules. This is crucial in dynamic environments where services can be added or removed frequently.
- Integration with Docker and Kubernetes: Traefik integrates seamlessly with Docker and Kubernetes to provide service discovery and load balancing for containerized applications. You can learn how to integrate your Go applications with these popular containerization and orchestration platforms.

5. Prometheus

Prometheus is a leading open-source monitoring system and time series database. Its codebase is a valuable resource for learning about:

- Metrics collection and storage: Prometheus collects and stores metrics from various sources, providing insights into system performance and health. You can learn how to instrument your Go applications to collect metrics and expose them to Prometheus.

- Alerting: Prometheus provides a powerful alerting system that can notify you of potential issues based on defined rules and thresholds. You can learn how to configure alerts and integrate them with notification systems.
- Time series data: Prometheus is designed to handle time series data efficiently, making it suitable for monitoring and analyzing trends over time. You can learn how to work with time series data in Go and build monitoring dashboards.

Where to Find These Projects

All these projects are hosted on GitHub:

- Docker: github.com/docker/docker
- Kubernetes: github.com/kubernetes/kubernetes
- etcd: github.com/etcd-io/etcd
- Traefik: github.com/traefik/traefik
- Prometheus: github.com/prometheus/prometheus

Tips for Analyzing Codebases

- Start with the README: The README file usually provides an overview of the project and instructions for building and running it.
- Explore the code structure: Look at the directory structure and file organization to understand how the project is structured.
- Read the documentation: Many projects have documentation that explains the design choices and implementation details.
- Focus on specific areas: If you're interested in a particular aspect (like concurrency or networking), focus on the parts of the code that deal with that area.
- Use debugging tools: Use debugging tools to step through the code and understand how it works.
- Contribute to the project: If you find a bug or have an improvement, consider contributing to the project. This is a

great way to learn and give back to the open-source community.

Studying these open-source Go projects, you can gain valuable insights into how experienced developers build production-ready backend systems. You can learn about best practices, architectural patterns, and common solutions to challenges you might encounter in your own projects.

13.2 Architectural Patterns and Best Practices

As you venture further into the world of backend development with Go, you'll encounter various architectural patterns and best practices that can guide you in building robust, maintainable, and scalable systems. These patterns and practices are like tried-and-true recipes for software development, offering solutions to common challenges and helping you structure your applications effectively.[1]

Think of it like building a house. You wouldn't just start stacking bricks randomly, would you? You would follow architectural plans and building codes to ensure that the house is structurally sound, functional, and aesthetically pleasing.[2] Similarly, architectural patterns and best practices provide a framework for building well-designed and reliable software systems.[3]

Let's explore some key architectural patterns and best practices that are particularly relevant for Go backend development.

Architectural Patterns

- Microservices: This pattern involves breaking down your application into smaller, independent services that communicate with each other.[4] Each service focuses on a specific business capability and can be developed, deployed, and scaled independently.[5] This promotes modularity, flexibility, and resilience.[6]

Example: An e-commerce application might have separate microservices for product catalog, order management, user accounts, and payment processing.[7]

- Layered Architecture: This pattern organizes your code into distinct layers, each with a specific responsibility.[8] Common layers include presentation (handling user interface), business logic (implementing core application logic), and data access (interacting with databases).[9] This separation of concerns makes your code easier to understand, maintain, and test.

Example: A web application might have a controller layer to handle HTTP requests, a service layer to implement business logic, and a repository layer to interact with the database.[10]

- Clean Architecture: This pattern emphasizes separating the core business logic of your application from infrastructure concerns like databases, frameworks, and user interfaces.[11] This makes your code more testable, portable, and independent of specific technologies.

Example: In a Clean Architecture, the core business logic is defined in use cases that are independent of the database or web framework used.[12]

- Domain-Driven Design (DDD): DDD focuses on modeling software based on the domain it represents, using concepts and terminology from the business domain.[13] This helps create a shared understanding between developers and domain experts and leads to software that better reflects the business needs.

Example: In a banking application, DDD might involve creating objects and methods that represent real-world banking concepts like accounts, transactions, and customers.

- CQRS (Command Query Responsibility Segregation): CQRS separates read and write operations in your application.[14] This can improve performance and scalability, especially in applications with a high volume of read operations.

Example: A social media application might use separate data models for reading user feeds (optimized for quick retrieval) and writing new posts (optimized for data consistency).

- Event-Driven Architecture: This pattern uses events to trigger actions and communicate between different parts of the system.[15] This promotes loose coupling and allows for asynchronous communication, improving scalability and responsiveness.

Example: An e-commerce application might publish an "Order Placed" event when a user places an order, triggering other services to perform actions like updating inventory, sending notifications, and processing payments.[16]

Best Practices

In addition to architectural patterns, there are several best practices that can guide you in building high-quality Go backend systems:

- Code Reusability: Create reusable components and libraries to avoid code duplication and improve maintainability.[17] This might involve creating packages for common functionalities like data access, logging, or error handling.
- Error Handling: Implement robust error handling to gracefully handle errors and provide informative feedback.

Use custom error types to provide more context and make error handling more specific.

- Logging: Use structured logging to record events and errors for debugging and monitoring. This involves logging data in a structured format (like JSON) that can be easily searched and analyzed.
- Testing: Write comprehensive tests (unit, integration, and E2E) to ensure code quality and prevent regressions.[18] Aim for high test coverage and use testing frameworks and tools to make your tests more effective.[19]
- Documentation: Provide clear and concise documentation to explain the code and its usage. This includes documenting APIs, code comments, and README files.

Real-World Examples

These architectural patterns and best practices are used extensively in real-world Go projects:

- Docker: Docker uses a layered architecture to separate concerns and a microservices architecture to decompose its functionality into independent services.
- Kubernetes: Kubernetes uses a microservices architecture, event-driven architecture, and various best practices like code reusability and comprehensive testing.
- etcd: etcd uses a distributed systems architecture, concurrency and synchronization techniques, and gRPC for communication.[20]

By understanding and applying these architectural patterns and best practices, you can build Go backend systems that are well-structured, maintainable, scalable, and resilient. They provide a solid foundation for creating high-quality software that meets the needs of your users and your business.[21]

13.3 Learning from Real-World Examples

As you progress on your journey to becoming a proficient Go backend developer, one of the most effective ways to accelerate your learning is to study real-world examples. Think of it like learning a new sport. You can read books and watch videos, but to truly master the game, you need to observe and analyze how professional athletes play. Similarly, by studying production-ready codebases, you gain valuable insights into how experienced developers apply concepts, solve problems, and build high-quality systems.

In this section, we'll explore how to effectively learn from real-world Go projects, extracting knowledge and inspiration to enhance your own development skills.

1. Choose the Right Projects

The Go ecosystem is vast, so it's important to choose projects that align with your interests and learning goals. Consider factors like:

- Project Size and Complexity: Start with smaller, well-documented projects to get a grasp of the fundamentals. As you gain confidence, you can explore larger and more complex codebases.
- Relevance to Your Interests: Choose projects that are relevant to the types of applications you want to build. If you're interested in web development, look for web frameworks or API projects. If you're interested in distributed systems, explore projects like etcd or Kubernetes.
- Code Quality: Look for projects with high code quality, good documentation, and active communities. These projects are more likely to demonstrate best practices and provide valuable learning opportunities.

2. Explore the Codebase

Once you've chosen a project, take some time to explore its codebase.

- Start with the README: The README file usually provides an overview of the project, instructions for building and running it, and links to further documentation.
- Understand the Project Structure: Examine the directory structure and file organization to get a sense of how the project is structured. Look for patterns and conventions that you can apply to your own projects.
- Identify Key Components: Identify the core components of the project and how they interact with each other. This might involve understanding the main data structures, algorithms, and communication patterns.
- Focus on Specific Areas: If you're interested in a particular aspect, like concurrency or database interactions, focus on the parts of the code that deal with that area.

3. Read the Documentation

Many open-source projects have excellent documentation that explains the design choices, implementation details, and usage examples. Take advantage of this documentation to gain a deeper understanding of the project.

- API Documentation: If the project exposes an API, study the API documentation to understand how to interact with it.
- Design Documents: Some projects have design documents that explain the overall architecture and design decisions.[1]
- Code Comments: Pay attention to code comments, as they can provide valuable insights into the code's purpose and functionality.[2]

4. Use Debugging Tools

Debugging tools can help you step through the code, inspect variables, and understand how the code executes.[3] This can be invaluable for understanding complex logic or identifying the cause of errors.

- Debuggers: Use a debugger like Delve to step through the code, set breakpoints, and inspect variables.[4]
- Logging: Add logging statements to your code to track the execution flow and understand the values of variables at different points.[5]

5. Ask Questions and Engage with the Community

Many open-source projects have active communities where you can ask questions, discuss the code, and learn from other developers.[6]

- Forums and Mailing Lists: Join forums or mailing lists related to the project to ask questions and participate in discussions.[7]
- Issue Trackers: Browse the project's issue tracker to see what bugs or feature requests are being discussed.
- Chat Channels: Some projects have chat channels (like Slack or Discord) where you can interact with other developers in real-time.

6. Contribute to the Project

Contributing to an open-source project is a fantastic way to learn and give back to the community.

- Start with Small Contributions: Begin with small contributions like fixing typos in documentation or adding tests.[8]
- Submit Bug Reports: If you find a bug, submit a detailed bug report to the project's issue tracker.
- Propose Feature Requests: If you have an idea for a new feature, propose it to the community.

- Submit Code Changes: As you gain confidence, you can contribute code changes to fix bugs or implement new features.

Real-World Examples

Many developers have learned and improved their skills by studying open-source projects:[9]

- New Contributors: Many new Go developers learn by contributing to smaller open-source projects to gain experience and build their portfolio.
- Experienced Developers: Experienced developers often study the code of popular projects like Docker and Kubernetes to learn about best practices and advanced techniques.
- Companies: Companies often use open-source projects as a foundation for their own products and services, learning from the design and implementation of these projects.[10]

By actively engaging with real-world Go projects, you can accelerate your learning, gain valuable insights, and become a more proficient backend developer.

Conclusion

You've reached the end of this journey through Go backend engineering. We've covered a lot of ground, from the fundamentals of the Go language to the intricacies of building cloud-native applications. You've learned how to write efficient and concurrent code, interact with databases, design RESTful APIs, secure your applications, and deploy them to the cloud with Docker and Kubernetes.

Go has proven itself to be a powerful and versatile language for backend development, offering a unique blend of performance, simplicity, and concurrency. Its growing ecosystem and strong community support make it an excellent choice for building modern, scalable, and maintainable backend systems.

As you continue your Go development journey, remember that learning is an ongoing process. Stay curious, explore new libraries and frameworks, and engage with the Go community. The world of backend development is constantly evolving, so embrace new challenges and continue to refine your skills.

Key Takeaways

- Go Fundamentals: Master the basics of Go syntax, data types, control flow, and concurrency.
- Backend Concepts: Understand core backend concepts like the client-server model, HTTP, RESTful APIs, and data serialization.
- Database Interactions: Learn how to interact with SQL and NoSQL databases, using both raw queries and ORMs.
- Microservices Architecture: Embrace the principles of microservices and learn how to design, build, and deploy microservices with Go.

- Security: Prioritize security by implementing authentication, authorization, and protection against common vulnerabilities.
- Testing and CI/CD: Adopt testing practices and implement continuous integration and continuous delivery to ensure code quality and streamline your development process.
- Performance Optimization: Use profiling, benchmarking, and performance tuning techniques to optimize your Go applications for speed and efficiency.
- Cloud-Native Development: Leverage cloud platforms, Docker, and Kubernetes to deploy and scale your applications in the cloud.
- Learning from Examples: Study open-source Go projects and real-world examples to learn from experienced developers and gain insights into best practices.

You now have the knowledge and tools to build robust, scalable, and secure backend systems with Go. Go forth, embrace the challenges of backend development, and create amazing applications that make a difference in the world.

www.ingramcontent.com/pod-product-compliance
Lightning Source LLC
LaVergne TN
LVHW081521050326
832903LV00025B/1565